esc

400 YEARS of COMPUTER HUMOR

Chris Miksanek

ISBN: 1434892484
EAN-13: 9781434892485

www.bamberbooks.com

For all the ones and zeros that made this possible.

Introduction to the 10th Edition[1]

My friend John Alarimo has the curtains from the film *Serpico* hanging in his apartment.

"They're very nice drapes," he told me. "The blood washed right out."

John was Dino De Laurentiis' right hand man, translating scripts into Italian—the director's preferred language—and serving as an assistant director on many of his films.

I met John in the late '80s when we were both called to jury duty.

He was a master storyteller.

On our frequent breaks we would walk up Hollywood Boulevard to find lunch and he would regale me with anecdotes on everything from the various obscure stars on which we stepped to his time as an A.D. in Rome on the classic film *Ben-Hur* where it sounded as if his #1 responsibility was to smuggle disposable cigarette lighters across the Alps from Switzerland.

John stayed behind the scenes most of the time though he did once acquiesce to De Laurentiis' prodding and do a last minute stand-in on *The Valachi Papers*. It was his only credited role (he's in the elevator scene behind Charles Bronson).

But I think I chucked most when he recounted an experience of his on the 1979 film *Hurricane*.

---

[1] Actually, it's the 2nd Edition, but as we say in the trade, there are 10 kinds of people: those who understand binary and those that don't.

"I remember taking Roman Polanski [the film's original director] to the airport for the weekend," John recalled. "He said 'I'll see you Monday.' We never saw him again."

Then, almost on cue, he shrugged.

So what does John have to do with this collection of information technology columns?

Everything. This book would not have been possible without him.

It was John who asked of the zine I was publishing at the time, "who buys that?" sparking an exchange that eventually directed me towards an untapped niche: computer humor.

From there was born *MISinformation: The first and only newsletter of computer humor.*

Computer humor had been around before *MISinformation*, mostly as filler in the various trades; PCs were not yet ubiquitous. Unfortunately, most of the entertainment was pretty sorry and consisted of either an authentic IBM "Mouse Balls" memo, a news story describing how Microsoft acquired something huge (e.g., "Microsoft Acquires the Catholic Church") or some variation of: Who's in charge of the computers at a monastery? The chip monk. Mutations of this lameness were tagged with "chocolate chips" and "chips and dip." Another went: which way did the Texas programmer go? He went data way.

These things are painful to type today, but are what passed for tech yuks back then.

I wanted to elevate computer humor and most of the time I like to think we did though there was the occasional interview with Art Linkeditor, Gomer Compiler, or two of the famed Radio City Diskettes: Kay and Meg (quips Kay, "Meg was always the dense one!"). Yes, if I had to do it all over again, I might have cut those as well as the news story about Elvis' email being marked "Return to Sender."

But I digress.

We did some good things, too. We reviewed entertainment software (one of my favorites was, naturally, a writing tool called "The Humor Processor") and we even spoofed other magazines like *InformationWeek* ("The new Cray 3 is so fast it can perform an infinite loop in 3 seconds") and *The National Enquirer* ("Says IBM 3090, 'I was a copier in previous life'").

Circulation was far from inspiring but we wrote as if it was and the newsletter caught the eye of some industry publications which eventually earned me a position as the humor columnist for the venerable IT journal *Datamation*.

There's "leading edge" and there's "bleeding edge." My column was "Over the Edge."

What began as a page of gag news stories would have been unremarkable were it not for my editor there at the time, Alden Hayashi. It was Alden who said, "These are funny, but you know what would be great? If you made some kind of point."

Alden denies having a role in transforming my writing from just a goof to something with a whiff of relevancy but his suggestion really was the missing link. The humor kept the reader engaged, but it was the point that stuck with them.

A lot has changed in the decade or so since the last column was published and while some of the humor here is vintage, the sentiments are timeless, for example:

> - When Bill Gates makes money, so do our 401ks
> - Vacation is a myth, the work will be waiting for you when you get back to your cubicle
> - The dream of a paperless society can never be realized until there is a way to do the *New York Times* crossword puzzle in the men's room

Of course, not everything reprinted here strived to make a point. Some of what follows is pure entertainment and the reader may have a dizzying time modulating between nods of concurrence and head shakes at the prospect that perhaps Shakespeare's prose was the basis for some of today's product manuals.

Still, it was all great fun to write and I hope, to read, as well.

Finally, I would be remiss were I not to acknowledge with gratitude the art of Daniel Guidera. Daniel was the original "Over the Edge" illustrator so it was a reflex to beg his help for the cover of this edition. He agreed and I am thrilled at the reunion. Daniel's work has been seen, among other places, in *Boy's Life*, *IBM Systems Magazine*, *MAD Magazine*, Target, Topps Stadium Club baseball cards, *Consumer Reports* and the iPad app "My Dad Drives A Roller Coaster Car."

Chris Miksanek, 2012

Foreword

I have never met Chris Miksanek. Yes, I've spoken with him over the phone countless times, and through the years we must have exchanged hundreds of e-mails. But I've never ever met the guy in person. So, as far as I know, he might not even exist. I do know one thing for certain, though, and that's this: Whoever has been writing his columns has a clever, playful wit that is as insightful as it is hilarious.

I was first introduced to Chris' humor in the mid 1990s. At the time, I was an editor with *Datamation*, a bi-weekly magazine that covered the IT industry. A fellow editor showed me some of Chris' writings, and I was immediately intrigued. Who is this guy? I asked. And after multiple phone conversations and e-mails with him, I was sure that Chris' unique voice had to be more prominently featured in the pages of *Datamation*. Soon, Chris was the regular contributor to the "Over the Edge" column, his humor bringing laughter to tens of thousands of readers every issue. His writing displayed an uncanny knack for good-naturedly poking fun at the many foibles and absurdities of the IT world. (Just start reading this book and you'll quickly see what I mean.)

Editing Chris' column was always a treat. In fact, I'd often save his column as the last thing I'd work on before shipping everything to the printer. It was my treat—a reward for having successfully slogged through reams of copy for the rest of the issue, which might have included long, technical feature articles about the latest IBM mainframes, the pros and cons of using Java applets, the most recent release of some unwieldy software package (ugh!). Yes, working on Chris' column was a sheer joy, not only because it meant that the editing for the upcoming issue was almost done but also because his humor never failed to make me chuckle. It was the perfect way to finish a grueling cycle of editorial work.

In a way, I rather like the fact that I've never actually met Chris. That way my mind can always imagine him in various ways. He is the IT guy who just upgraded my Office software at work, or the networking specialist who changed the router in my building last month, or the technical guru who recommended an enterprise resource planning package for my organization, or the chip designer who is developing a future generation of semiconductors that will power the next laptop computer that I buy. For me, Chris will always exist in the ubiquitous silicon ether of our Digital Age. He is everywhere. And boy is he funny.

—Alden M. Hayashi
Former executive editor of *Datamation*

Nietzsche: "The mainframe is dead."

SYSOP: "I just suspended Nietzsche's userid."

Bill Gates needs more money

When the NASDAQ took a dip a while back and Microsoft's Bill Gates lost eleven billion dollars in one week, some jealous competitors (is it grammatically correct to have the words "Microsoft" and "competitor" in the same sentence?) asked the *Believe It or Not!* museum if they could borrow the world's smallest violin to play him a tune.

Indeed, few shed tears for Redmond's fortunate son.

But a custodian in Minneapolis wept. So did an administrative assistant in Albuquerque. And a personal shopper in Coral Gables bawled her eyes out until they were bloodshot.

None of these people had ever met Bill Gates, and they couldn't care less if he uses coupons when he goes shopping. They wailed because last year *their* Microsoft stock touched $120 a share, and this year, when the Justice Department made a move to help run the company "better," their stock plunged to as low as $60.

Bill Gates can afford to lose a third of his net worth, but the average person's 401k, IRA, KEOGH, or rainy day mutual fund can't. And most regular people are getting a little irregular over it.

"Monopoly, antitrust, noncompetitive practices ... these are just big words," says Jay O'Melvey, who is not an economist, but is president of the Oklahoma chapter of the Alan Greenspan Fan Club. "Basically, you have the largest organization in the country, the U.S. government—itself, probably the most fiscally irresponsible—telling one of the most successful companies, Microsoft, to throttle back. This all flies in the face of a free economy. The government supports, and in many cases subsidizes, weak companies and fights strong ones."

Of course it's not just regular people who have their eyes on Gates' strongbox. Institutional investors, like pension fund directors and insurance companies, also wring their handkerchiefs as stocks palpitate.

And it's not just Gates' tollbooth change, which could feed the entire country of Borneo for a year, that's under the microscope. This year, Larry Ellison's wallet moved to a close second from carry-on size to mandatory check-in (a moot analogy because he flies his own $38-million Gulfstream).

The point is, when today's technology robber barons prosper, we all do. For some, the prosperity translates to a higher-valued retirement portfolio; for others, there are ancillary benefits. Last year, for instance, philanthropic donations were at an all-time high. "I don't know how my business could have survived last year without so many generous donations to my clients," says Soho's Bruce Babcock, who supplies animal manure to artists in his area. "This year, though, it's a whole other story. But I'm optimistic. I've ordered four more potbellied pigs."

More to the point, you're probably asking yourself what *you* can do to make Bill Gates and his billionaire club pals richer, which means help them help you.

Well, for the most part, you've already contributed. You've made Windows the most popular operating system, Intel the most popular processor, and, well, we have no explanation for Price-line.com's success except that maybe they found a whole colony of mushroom smokers who thought it was amusing to see William Shatner's toupee flap as he does his Pete Townsend imitation.

But you can do more! For instance:

Whatever brand PC you have, it's time for an upgrade. In fact, it's always time. Why not consider buying the latest from Dell Computer Corp.? (NASDAQ: DELL). Billionaire Michael Dell will thank you and so will the grandmother in Denver who has used the stock's appreciation to help pay for her prescription medication the past four years. And if you already have a PC, why not consider buying a Sun Microsystems, Inc. (NASDAQ: SUNW) UltraSPARC Workstation?

Sure, Scott McNealy will appreciate it, but so will an orphanage in Milwaukee that was the beneficiary of 50 shares of the company's stock. Of course, if you have both a PC and a workstation, you could add an Apple Computer, Inc. (NASDAQ: AAPL) iMac; that would please the heck out of Steve Jobs and make a lot of other people happy, not the least of whom is an investment club of retired postal workers in Phoenix.

Looking for something on the Net? Start where many advertisers hope you will: Yahoo! (NASDAQ: YHOO). *Wunderkinder* David Filo and Jerry Yang will thank you, and so will the carpenter in Indianapolis who has been accumulating shares at the rate of five per month to save for his daughter's college education. And if what you're looking for is a book, Jeff Bezos hopes you'll shop @ Amazon.com (NASDAQ: AMZN) as does the paperboy in DeKalb who owns five shares though the ILUTMA (Illinois Uniform Transfers to Minors Act) account that his father maintains for him.

DSL and cable ISPs are nice, but Steve Case still hopes you'll consider AOL, Inc. (NYSE: AOL); so does a nurse in Austin, Texas, for whom liberation from her twenty-two year bedpan cleaning tour of duty is just one more stock split away. And speaking of things you may not need, why not take a weekend to clean out the attic, basement, and/or cellar and post all that useless stuff on eBay (NASDAQ: EBAY)? Pierre Omidyar will appreciate it, but not nearly as much as Mr. Corcoran's senior economics class at Polk High School in Joplin, Missouri. Their grade is based on the performance of a virtual portfolio and they're bullish on eBay because, as one student reported, "after thorough analysis, we've concluded they have some cool stuff there."

You get the idea. The point of this all isn't to recommend any particular stocks in the technology sector. You can only determine what's right for your portfolio by consulting a certified financial planner or dart board.

The point is to try to ground the negative image companies acquire when their figureheads become a little too prosperous. Bill Gates is just one of the more than three million Microsoft shareholders. Many of the others are just average people who get up, go to work, and then come home and watch Regis. When Gates prospers, so do they.

Yes, it's true that sometimes business is hardball; and, yes, we have a long way to go before we're a functioning altruistic utopia. But that's capitalism, baby, and it's groovy, yeah!

... and then there was ...

> ... the sentimental UNIX programmer who still had the first .MAK file he'd ever made.

A stronger encryption strategy

Keeping ahead of the hacker curve when encryption algorithms are becoming increasingly ineffective

Whether you maintain corporate ledgers or confidential customer information, you must protect that sensitive data from prying eyes. Users often turn to encryption for assured privacy and security. But how good is today's encryption? While modern technology produces more secure encryption algorithms, hackers, armed with powerful processors, are often following right on the heels of these advances. Indeed, it is difficult, if not impossible, to stay one step ahead.

Off-the-shelf applications, it turns out, may not be the best solution, either. Recent disclosures of back doors into some of the applications companies rely on for data security have left many IS managers subscribing to the philosophy that "if you want something done right, do it yourself."

Developing and implementing a data security strategy of one's own is not, as some believe, rocket science. Contrary to popular belief, the goal of encryption is not to secure data forever, but only for that period of time until the data is no longer useful.

Consider this scenario: a system user's password expires every thirty days. Therefore, a password encryption algorithm that requires thirty-one days to crack is just as effective as one that requires thirty-one years to crack. Of course, you could argue that the algorithm that takes thirty-one days to crack today will take only thirty-one microseconds to crack with next year's hardware. And you would be correct.

So how can you stay ahead of the hacker curve when encryption algorithms are becoming increasingly ineffective? The answer is to choose a different course. Don't try to computationally out-power them. Rather, out-maneuver them. In boxing parlance, it's the rope-a-dope.

Build a better secret decoder ring
and the NSA will beat a path to your door

The most primitive encryption is known as simple substitution. A simple substitution algorithm replaces one character or digit with another. For example, if N = 5, I = C, C = E, K = N, E= T, and L = S, then "5CENTS" equals "NICKEL." But that's obvious, and it is the fundamental weakness of the simple substitution algorithms. It doesn't take much programmatic "looking" to break them. Using *frequency analysis*—comparing the number of times a substituted character occurs in ciphertext with the frequency in which a character occurs in a large body of text—simple-substitution algorithms are easy to crack.

To defeat frequency analysis attacks, expand the character relations. Instead of a one-to-one correspondence, assign a complete word to a character, for example, "A" is for "apple," "J" is for "jacks." You can make the encryption even more secure by assigning entire phrases to individual characters as illustrated in the code sample in Figure 1.

Phrase-level encoding can be further expanded so that phrases are substituted with other phrases. "Knock three times on the ceiling" might mean "if you want me." "Twice on the pipe," "if the answer is no." And so on. For extremely sensitive data, consider making the algorithm virtually intractable by disguising it. Add the extension .DES or .RSA to the encrypted filename and send any would-be infiltrator on a protracted wild-goose chase.

Security by obscurity

Another method to secure sensitive data is to maintain it in a format other than text. Where do you store valuables at home? Behind a painting in the living room, of course. Where can you hide

```
dec_str = ''                        /* initialize dec_str*/
do while length(enc_str) > 0        /* decrypt enc_str   */
   select

      when substr(enc_str,1,1) = 'L' then
         dec = 'for the way you look at me'
      when substr(enc_str,1,1) = 'O' then
         dec = 'for the only one I see'
      when substr(enc_str,1,1) = 'V' then
         dec = 'very, very extraordinary'
      when substr(enc_str,1,1) = 'E' then
         dec = 'even more than anyone that you adore can'

      otherwise
         dec = substr(enc_str,1,1)  /* not a known phrase */
      end /* select */

      dec_str = dec_str||dec        /* build dec_str      */
      enc_str = substr(enc_str,2)   /* adjust enc_str     */

      end /* do while loop */

say 'decrypted string:' dec str  /* echo decrypted str */
```

Figure 1: Sample code that decrypts a phrase-level simple-substitution-encoded file.

valuables on a workstation? Behind a paint file. Frequency analysis is ineffective against graphics files. Such a file boasts no normal character distributions or discernible word patterns.

Figure 2 illustrates such a graphically protected password file. Rename the extension to prevent accidental opening, and rename the file to dissuade purposeful access. RECIPES.TXT, for example, is unlikely to be bothered with.

What a fool believes

Of course, the integrity of data can never be 100 percent assured and sometimes the best offense is a gaping hole in the defense that leads directly to a roach motel. Good, old-fashioned disinformation can be used to ferret out the hacker.

On networks with no external access, create an easily accessible file with a too-good-to-be-true file name as bait. PAYROLL.TXT, for instance, is a magnet for snoopers. Once the file is set up, the game begins. Can you identify the network account of the perpetrator before they learn it was a setup and discover that PAYROLL.TXT is really the Microsoft Project file that keeps track of whose turn it is to buy donuts? The unknown outcome of the entrapment is why IT is such an exciting field.

If your network has external access, the easiest way to identify who is trying to compromise your security is to seed a "magnet" file with lesser-known names from the Ten-Most-Wanted list. If your identity thief shows up at a bank unwittingly claiming to be one of those felons, or tries to cash a postal money order, the FBI will do the rest.

Lock your car, take your keys

Effective encryption doesn't require mathematically complex algorithms or NSA-powered processors. It just requires cunning and simple programming skills. Exploit the resources currently available in your organization to secure sensitive data by implementing wily methods to throw your interlopers off course.

References

- *DES for Dummies*, J. David Zuda, IDG Books.
- *The Complete Idiot's Guide to the National Security Agency*, Professor Roy Hinkley, Castaway Books
- *Oh Behave: Austin Powers' Guide to Counter-Intelligence*, Shag Press, Ltd.

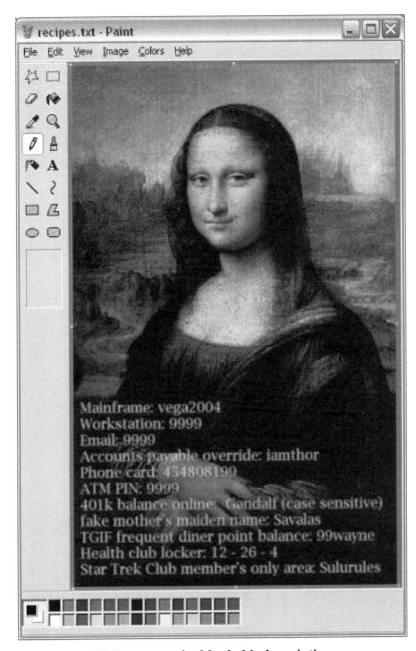

Figure 2: Try hiding your valuables behind a painting

Jokes they might tell if the big names played the main room at COMDEX ...

> **George Carlin:** "Let's say you phone Alan Turing; how do you know if *he* answers or if you just got his machine?"

More made-up computer jokes on page 51.

Code-3: real life PC dramatizations

Gil Gerrard hosts this drama about real life rescue missions of the genre *Rescue 911* and *COPS*. This segment, titled "The One That Got Away," never aired and was instead replaced at the last minute with the story of two white-water rafters stranded on the rocks after attempting to retrieve a cooler filled with Budweiser. No explanation was given for the last-minute episode switch.

FADE IN:
INT. MTO BULLPEN. GIL IS STANDING IN FRONT OF SOME TERMINALS. IN B.G., TAPE DRIVES ARE REELING WITH ACTIVITY.

> GIL
> The men and women of the Help Desk
> handle hundreds of calls for help
> twenty-four hours a day,
> three-hundred sixty-five days a year.
> Some are just user errors, others are
> genuine application crap-outs. When
> department data is on the line, the
> experts of the help desk get called in.
> Join us now for this exciting
> dramatization.

FADE OUT.

FADE IN:
INT. INTERVIEW ROOM.

JOE SPIVAK--HEAD SHOT AGAINST BLACK B.G.

> JOE
> I was reading a magazine when the call
> came in from the Accounts Receivables
> department. This guy was wailing like a
> baby. "I deleted it, I deleted it." I could
> hardly get his name or userid. Luckily,
> we have those telephones that display
> the extension number of the caller.
> I determined that the call came from
> office 817.

CUT TO:
INT. MTO BULLPEN.

> GIL
> The call came from office 817. Clear at the
> other end of the building.

CUT TO:
INT. INTERVIEW ROOM.

> JOE
> I immediately dispatched Luke, who was on
> break.

CUT TO:
INT. BREAK ROOM. LUKE IS SITTING BEHIND A LUNCH ROOM
TABLE, THE NEWSPAPER IS SPREAD-OUT.

HE IS ABOUT TO LIGHT A CIGARETTE WHEN THE PHONE RINGS.
HE GETS UP, CROSSES ROOM TO PHONE, PICKS UP RECEIVER.

> LUKE
> It's working as designed.
>
> > (Listens for a moment.
> > His expression changes.)
>
> Jesus! I'll be right there.

LUKE QUICKLY EXITS. RETURNS. GATHERS UP NEWSPAPER. EXITS
AGAIN.

CUT TO:
INT. MTO BULLPEN

GIL

The men had to hurry because when a
frantic user deletes a file, time is of the
essence. A user can do more damage by
trying to recover the file himself. The
condition is generally reversible with a
good utility program unless the dufus
reallocates the disk block.

CUT TO:
INT. INTERVIEW ROOM.

JOE

I had to keep him talking. As long as I had
him on the phone I knew he wouldn't be
screwing with his PC and we stood a good
chance of saving his file.

CUT TO:
INT. MTO BULLPEN.

GIL

This would give Luke the valuable time he
needed to get to Office 817.

CUT TO:
INT. INTERVIEW ROOM.

JOE

I told him everything's gonna be OK. That
help was on the way. In the mean time, I
asked him what he was working on. Turns out
he was working on a spreadsheet for half of
the day before someone came in and
accidentally stepped on the master
power-button on his power strip.

CUT TO:
INT. MTO BULLPEN.

GIL

To make matters worse, the user didn't do
frequent saves, so the best the boys could
hope for was to somehow massage the
spreadsheet's temporary file into something
usable.

CUT TO:
INT. INTERVIEW ROOM.

> JOE
> I asked him what he did, and he said he
> called the guy who stepped on his power
> strip a dumb son of a ...

SFX: BEEP

> JOE
> (cont'd)
> Then he said he powered his PC back on,
> that he was using OS/2 so he figured in the
> eight or so minutes it took to boot he would
> call us. In a split second, it hit me. This
> guy's in trouble.

CUT TO:
INT. MTO BULLPEN.

> GIL
> The user was in trouble because the
> spreadsheet application would do its own
> housekeeping and automatically delete any
> temporary files on startup.

CUT TO:
INT. INTERVIEW ROOM.

> JOE
> To make matters worse, the guy told me he
> had an alias of the spreadsheet application
> in his startup folder! I tried to sound
> convincing when I told him...

CUT TO:
INT. HELP DESK CUBICLE. JOE IS ON THE PHONE WITH THE USER.

> JOE
> (cont'd)
> It's OK, someone's on the way.

CUT TO:
INT. MTO BULLPEN.

                    GIL
        The trek for Luke should have only taken
        two minutes, but he ran into a delay...

CUT TO:
EXT. MEN'S ROOM. LUKE EXITS.

CUT TO:
INT. MTO BULLPEN.

                    GIL
        Time was running out.

CUT TO:
INT. INTERVIEW ROOM.

                    JOE
        From the voice on the phone, I could tell
        I was losing him ...

CUT TO:
SCREEN GRAPHIC: TAPE RECORDER REELS SLOWLY TURNING.

                    USER
                (SFX: 911 TAPE)
        Hurry. My review, my work ... due date ...
        Where's the help, Holy God in heaven, where's
        the help?!

CUT TO:
INT. MTO BULLPEN.

                    GIL
        Where *was* the help?

CUT TO:
INT. SECURITY DESK AREA.
LUKE IS WORKING OVER THE SHOULDER OF AN ATTRACTIVE
FEMALE SECURITY GUARD, HELPING HER WITH HER PC.

                    LUKE
        No, no, here, like this.

LUKE PUTS HIS HAND ON HERS AND GUIDES HER MOUSE.

                              LUKE
                            (cont'd)
              Drag it like this when the apples fall
              from the trees; get that acorn before the
              flying squirrel. See?

                         SECURITY GUARD
              Gee, I've never been to level four before!

CUT TO:
INT. MTO BULLPEN.

                              GIL
              Meanwhile, the user's desktop was starting
              to build.

CUT TO:
INT. INTERVIEW ROOM.

                              JOE
              The guy was getting frantic, his
              applications were starting.

INT. USER'S OFFICE.
LUKE ARRIVES.

CUT TO:
INT. MTO BULLPEN.

                              GIL
              Luke immediately pressed the power-off
              button to halt any further damage. He
              surveyed the room. A crowd had gathered.
              Luke needed a coffee. He told the user he
              would be back in a few minutes. That the
              user should just leave the computer alone.

              Later in the afternoon, Luke came back.
              There was a boot problem, and OS/2
              wouldn't come up. In the end, Luke had to
              reformat the user's disk; not only did the
              user lose the morning's updates, but all
              of them since his backup the week before.

CUT TO:
INT. INTERVIEW ROOM.

> JOE
> Not all of our stories have happy endings.

CUT TO:
INT. MTO BULLPEN.

> GIL
> Next up, a construction worker hangs
> upside down for six hours as rescue
> workers rush to find all two dollars and
> sixty cents in change that fell out of
> his pockets onto the ground thirty
> stories below!

FADE OUT.

Epistemological philosophers ...

... in Washington State are asking if Microsoft could create a document so large that even Word could not open it. This on the rumor that Bill Gates' pre-nuptial agreement was written on an IBM 3090 mainframe using GML.

Quitting with panache

If you're an average IT pro, you'll switch jobs six times in your career. This is according to Leo DeVoe, who is not an industry analyst, but he's written a nice freeware random number generator.

And you don't need a Magic 8 Ball to tell you that the times, they are a-changin'. Our industry has never had as many employment opportunities as it does now. But while most of the focus has been on how you can secure a new, more lucrative position, little ink has been devoted to severing the ties of your old one. "Indeed," DeVoe says, "six out of five people don't know how to quit effectively."

While DeVoe's statistical generator may not be ready for prime time, his message is. "Your termination should speak for you," he says. "It should be your *magnum opus*."

Here, then, is your guide to a purposeful resignation.

Don't burn bridges ...

"Leave on good terms" has always been the mantra, the rationale being that you may need a good reference or want to come back some day. DeVoe says that's all bunk. "In these litigious times, old employers are limited in what they can divulge," he says. "If you need good references, use your friends, colleagues, and fake personalities you create on Facebook or LinkedIn." And as far as coming back, DeVoe says, "rehire status" is HR propaganda—only two of 1,000 employees boomerang back to their old jobs.

... Unless parting isn't such sweet sorrow

You typically take a new job because you don't like the old one. Maybe it doesn't pay what you think you're worth, your department was inequitably funded, or management didn't know its cache from its elbow. Whatever the reason, you need to get it off your chest at the exit interview so you'll be able to start your next job trek with a clean mental slate.

But perhaps you're a bit intimidated. Maybe you think that during your exit interview, HR will desperately promise you things will change. They will point out how just recently the company break room was stocked with those cool colored flex-straws and a counter-top reverse osmosis drinking water spigot. More likely, you just can't find the words to express your contempt.

That's where we come in. We can't liberate you from the gulag, but we can help you make them sorry they soured you.

So take a deep breath and find some glasses like Michael Douglas wore in the movie *Falling Down*, because you're about to make the *Reservoir Dogs* look like *101 Dalmatians*; you're a volcano about to go Pompeii on the place. By the time you're done getting your message across, a WWF Smackdown is going to look like a quilting bee. But enough with the analogies (though we could go on like Jimmy Stewart filibustering in *Mr. Smith Goes to Washington*). You have a few critical assignments to complete before you're escorted out.

Let's start with Krazy Glue, which, next to onion-flavored chewing gum and itching powder, is probably the most useful tool for exacting revenge. Put a dab on:

- the ENTER key of any target workstation so it can't be pressed.
- all the current workstation network cards just before the scheduled hardware upgrade.
- the server backup tapes so they won't spin when a restore is necessary.
- the videoconference camera focus knob, set to "infinity."
- the CD-ROM tray of the machine that runs your mission critical applications so when emergency maintenance needs to be applied, they'll all share a hearty laugh.
- whatever else you think will leave them remembering you fondly.

Huh? You still have some Krazy Glue left? Boy, they sure get a lot into those little tubes, don't they? And it would just be a damn shame for any of it to go to waste. Well, why not take it down to the corporate fitness room and apply it sparingly to the bottom of the ten-pound barbells that your favorite manager uses to impress the administrative help?

If you're into sophomoric office pranks (it's not a prerequisite, by the way) you can take the hinge pins off the lunchroom fridge. Move the condiment bottles to the door shelves first for added impact. It's a merry half-hour clean up. Or at least normally it would be a half-hour, but you've taken care to slash the bottoms of all the lunchroom trash bags. Sure it's shameful, but you're making a statement here, so who has time for guilt? Oh, and poke a few holes in the coffee filters. It adds texture to the morning brew.

On your way out of the lunchroom, stop by the mailroom, drop a dead fish in an interoffice envelope (mullet, if you can get it, but anything fresh is better than frozen) and address it to some imaginary person in a department that was eliminated in the last reorg. By the time the envelope gets passed around a few times, it'll take on a personality of its own, albeit a foul one. It's hard to imagine that you began your career there as a happy cog in the wheel, isn't it?

And don't limit your tirade to just one person or department. You can change system messages and expound your political views to the entire organization. For example, "Management's move to deny domestic partner benefits to Palm Pilots is but a further oppression of the proletarian technical staff ... Welcome to OS/400 V4R2." Of course, if you have access to source code, you can do even more damage.

They've probably grown accustomed to bugs in the software. But what about bugs in the hardware? With the aid of a mail-order scientific supply company that doesn't ask too many questions, you can dump a pack of dung beetle larvae, maggots, or cicada eggs (the latter, a seventeen year "time release" type) inside a warm RS/6000 and then read about it in the trade magazines long after you've left.

As a final act of impudence, open a standard diskette, replace the magnetic disk inside with 600-grit sandpaper, reseal it, and label it "Head Cleaner." Leave it on your superior's desk. That's what he gets for promising you a six-figure salary and not telling you about the leading zeros.

The point of all this isn't to launch your own personal jihad. In fact, there's nothing nefarious at all about it. To those colleagues you leave behind you owe an accurate account of why you're moving on. In time, if enough people, err, "express" their discontent, things may change for the better. But even if they don't, for you, it's cathartic. And if your old management can't appreciate that, there's always dogdoo.com.

Crystal-clear exit interview ambiguity

Exit interviews are rife with noncritical, noncommittal *non sequitur*. Most are also noneffective nonsensical nomenclature.

This is your one time to lay it all on the line and possibly affect change for your former colleagues. But what do you typically do? Speak in code. Too often, though, that "code" is misinterpreted and you're tagged as just another malcontent.

Here are some examples of the crucial need to clearly articulate your reasons for leaving.

What you say: "I'm leaving to pursue a new opportunity."

What they hear: "Jumping for the money. This employee can't be pleased."

What you really mean: "The new opportunity I'm leaving to pursue is the reclamation of my dignity, which you've slowly stripped me of over these past twelve years of loyal service. It was either that or open a vein."

What you say: "I'm starting my own business."

What they hear: "This employee has delusions of grandeur, and wants to be CEO of our company. This employee can't be pleased."

What you really mean: "There was time when this organization operated as an *esprit de corps*. There was synergy, and we were each able to make an impact. But we've grown into a corporation replete with overhead. Process and administration have taken precedence over innovation, and if you all don't see that, you must be sniffing toner!"

What you say: "My spouse has been transferred out of town, so we need to relocate."

What they hear: "Counter-offer of colorful flex-straws and a countertop reverse-osmosis drinking water spigot was rebuffed. This employee can't be pleased."

What you really mean: "My wife, I think I'll keep her. She empowers me to tell you all to take the pipe!"

When software acts like visiting relatives

To: RitchieGecko@respectmyprivacy.com
From: raymondbouchard@relativelyeffectivesecuretechnologies.com
Reply To: wecareaboutyourresponse@mungedbeyonddelivery.com
Subject: Thank you for downloading Asbestos 1.1
Date: April 1, 2001 14:05:13 -0600

Hello Ritchie Gecko,
Thank you for downloading Asbestos 1.1 Personal Edition. We share a common concern that Internet privacy and security is of paramount importance. With Asbestos protection, you can surf with confidence.

I also invite you to upgrade your free Personal Edition to Asbestos Pro for only $29.95. Check our web site for details.

Best Regards,
Raymond Bouchard, President
RelativelyEffectiveSecureTechologies, Inc.

P.S. As a courtesy, we have subscribed you to the relativelyeffectivesecuretechologies e-newsletter as RitchieGecko@respectmyprivacy.com. To unsubscribe, visit our web site and navigate through a few simple panels until you've got it figured out.

To: RitchieGecko@respectmyprivacy.com
From: salesandsupport@relativelyeffectivesecuretechnologies.com
Reply To: wecareaboutyourresponse@mungedbeyonddelivery.com
Subject: relativelyeffectivesecuretechologies e-newsletter
Date: April 1, 2001 14:05:14 -0600

Ritchie,
As a subscriber to the relativelyeffectivesecuretechologies e-newsletter, we're offering you an opportunity to upgrade to Asbestos Pro for only $29.95. Asbestos Pro offers many security options that your

Personal Edition does not. For example, while some freeware firewalls, Asbestos Personal Edition, for instance, log web surfing habits and forward that information to a central repository, Asbestos Pro does not. Upgrade today.

Best Regards,
Raymond Bouchard, President
RelativelyEffectiveSecureTecholologies, Inc.

To: RitchieGecko@respectmyprivacy.com
From: raymondbouchard@relativelyeffectivesecuretechnologies.com
Reply To: wecareaboutyourresponse@mungedbeyonddelivery.com
Subject: Uninstall Confirmation
Date: April 2, 2001 09:57:07 -0600

Ritchie,
We are saddened by your uninstall of Asbestos Personal Edition, which we detected via our uninstall utility. We feel that we have one of the most effective tools on the market and know you'll give us a second chance to prove it. That's why the uninstall utility has reinstalled your copy of Asbestos Personal Edition. If you really want to uninstall our product, execute the uninstall utility again. But if you believe, as we do, that Asbestos is the best free firewall out there, you'll want to keep it operating! And to make sure you have the opportunity for even more protection and flexibility, we're extending a special *Welcome Back* offer. Upgrade now to Asbestos Pro for only $29.95. Visit our site for details.

Thanks for giving us a second chance,
Raymond Bouchard, President
RelativelyEffectiveSecureTecholologies, Inc.

To: RitchieGecko@respectmyprivacy.com
From: raymondbouchard@ relativelyeffectivesecuretechnologies.com
Reply To: wecareaboutyourresponse@mungedbeyonddelivery.com
Subject: Uninstall Confirmation
Date: April 2, 2001 10:12:22 -0600

Ritchie,
We are saddened by your uninstall of Asbestos Personal Edition, which we detected via our uninstall utility. We feel that we have one of the most effective tools on the market and know you'll give us a second chance to prove it. That's why the uninstall utility has reinstalled your copy of Asbestos Personal Edition. If you really want to uninstall our product, execute the uninstall utility again. But if you believe, as we

do, that Asbestos is the best free firewall out there, you'll want to keep it operating! And to make sure you have the opportunity for even more protection and flexibility, we're extending a special *welcome back* offer. Upgrade now to Asbestos Pro for only $29.95. Visit our site for details.

Thanks for giving us a second chance,
Raymond Bouchard, President
RelativelyEffectiveSecureTechologies, Inc.

To: RitchieGecko@respectmyprivacy.com
From: raymondbouchard@ relativelyeffectivesecuretechnologies.com
Reply To: wecareaboutyourresponse@mungedbeyonddelivery.com
Subject: Welcome to Windows XP
Date: April 2, 2001 11:19:50 -0600

Welcome to Windows XP. We've detected a Windows reinstall on your PC, and to maintain the integrity of your new operating environment, Asbestos Personal Edition has reinstalled itself from a hidden and protected DLL. We know you'll appreciate this functionality and recognize it as just one example of how relativelyeffectivesecuretechnologies.com takes your security seriously. However, if for some reason you want Asbestos Personal Edition completely eradicated from your machine—for instance, if you're upgrading to Asbestos Pro at our special *Welcome to Windows XP* rate of $29.95—visit our web site for a list of Asbestos Pro's features, one of which is the Personal Edition pristine uninstall option.

Enjoy Windows XP and Asbestos,
Raymond Bouchard, President
RelativelyEffectiveSecureTechologies, Inc.

To: RitchieGecko@respectmyprivacy.com
From: salesandsupport@relativelyeffectivesecuretechnologies.com
Reply To: wecareaboutyourresponse@mungedbeyonddelivery.com
Subject: Web surfing report for April 2
Date: April 3, 2001 00:00:01 -0600

Ritchie,
When you downloaded Asbestos Personal Edition, by not opting-out (clicking the radio button that toggles between *opt-out* and *begin download*) you indicated you wanted a daily report of your web-surfing activities transmitted to our partner marketing organizations. You may

disable this option in Asbestos Pro, but unfortunately, we haven't implemented that functionality yet in the Personal Edition. While many users appreciate our monitoring of their surfing habits, a very small number do not. Though recent legal action is in appeal, we are voluntarily complying with an injunction sought by those who find such logging invasive. To those few, we make a special offer to upgrade to Asbestos Pro for only $29.95. See our web page for details.

Based on your browsing yesterday, our partner marketing organizations believe the following sites might be of interest:

> www.viagraherbalalternatives.com
> www.diplomamill.edu/PhDsforadollar
> www.nudecartooncharacters.com/bettyandveronica/

Type to you again tomorrow,
The Marketing Department,
RelativelyEffectiveSecureTechologies, Inc.

To: RichGeckoNOSPAM@respectmyprivacy.com
From: salesandsupport@relativelyeffectivesecuretechnologies.com
Reply To: wecareaboutyourresponse@mungedbeyonddelivery.com
Subject: We Found You
Date: April 3, 2001 09:41:13 -0600

Rich,
Did you know that each day, hundreds of thousands of Internet users change their email addresses without notifying vendors who provide valuable services like alerting you to discounted upgrade offers? Thanks to the packet sniffing technology embedded in Asbestos Personal Edition (which is, by default, always enabled) we were able to detect that you changed your email address and as a courtesy have shared that information with our marketing partners to ensure that you continue to receive offers of interest to you. No thanks necessary. That's the kind of service and support you get with relativelyeffectivesecuretechnologies.com.

Incidentally, packet-sniffing can be disabled in Asbestos Pro, and if you upgrade now, you'll pay only $29.95. Visit our web site for details.

Regards,
The Helpdesk,
RelativelyEffectiveSecureTecholgies, Inc.

P.S. By the way, you look great in the robe you swiped from the Hilton. But to keep your fashion shows private, why not upgrade to Asbestos Pro, the only firewall that ensures your webcam streams are seen only by those whom you intend?

To: RichGeckoNOSPAM@respectmyprivacy.com
From: raymondbouchard@relativelyeffectivesecuretechnologies.com
Reply To: wecareaboutyourresponse@mungedbeyonddelivery.com
Subject: Uninstall Confirmation
Date: April 3, 2001 09:44:51 -0600

Rich,
We are saddened by your uninstall of Asbestos Personal Edition, which we detected via our uninstall utility. We feel that we have one of the most effective tools on the market and know you'll give us a second chance to prove it. That's why the uninstall utility has reinstalled your copy of Asbestos Personal Edition. If you really want to uninstall our product, execute the uninstall utility again. But if you believe, as we do, that Asbestos is the best free firewall out there, you'll want to keep it operating! And to make sure you have the opportunity for even more protection and flexibility, we're extending a special *welcome back* offer. Upgrade now to Asbestos Pro for only $29.95. Visit our site for details.

Thanks for giving us a second chance,
Raymond Bouchard, President
RelativelyEffectiveSecureTechologies, Inc.

To: RichGeckoNOSPAM@respectmyprivacy.com
From: salesandsupport@relativelyeffectivesecuretechnologies.com
Reply To: wecareaboutyourresponse@mungedbeyonddelivery.com
Subject: HD Formatting Tech Tip #18
Date: April 3, 2001 10:01:33 -0600

Rich,
You recently formatted your hard drive and reinstalled Windows XP. Sometimes that's what it takes to clean up every file or registry entry that many pesky applications leave behind. But, as you know, relativelyeffectivesecuretechnologies.com takes your security serious. While reinstalling an operating system, there is a window of opportunity for a system violation. To thwart such hack-attacks, we've taken comprehensive technical measures (patent pending) to ensure we are reinstalled along with your operating system. For Asbestos Personal Edition users, we believe this is appropriate. However because power users want more control over their reinstallations, Asbestos Pro permits the auto-reinstall option to be disabled. Take advantage of our *Welcome to Windows XP* special promotion and upgrade today for only $29.95. Visit our site for details.

Regards,
The Helpdesk,
RelativelyEffectiveSecureTechologies, Inc.

To: RichGeckoNOSPAM@respectmyprivacy.com
From: raymondbouchard@ relativelyeffectivesecuretechnologies.com
Reply To: wecareaboutyourresponse@mungedbeyonddelivery.com
Subject: Thank you for upgrading to Asbestos Pro!
Date: April 3, 2001 11:19:05 -0600

Hello Rich Gecko,
Thank you for upgrading to our full-featured Asbestos Pro. Be assured that your privacy and security is our mission, and by purchasing our product, you've selected the best of the breed.

Now that your Internet surfing is safe and secure, it's time to turn your attention to other system vulnerabilities. For instance, did you know that just by reading this email, you may have unleashed a virus that could spread to all your friends and render their PCs useless—erasing all the files on their hard drive except, of course, for the Asbestos Personal Edition auto-reinstall DLL?

Such functionality can also be used for good operations, as well. As a valued Asbestos Pro user, we've made things easy for you. By opening this email, you have just installed a free version of relativelyeffective-securetechnologies.com's AmoxicilRX 1.0 Personal Edition virus detection software. A copy has also been distributed to everyone in your address book. We hope you'll email with confidence knowing AmoxicilRX 1.0 Personal Edition is hard at work. And as a special welcome to AmoxicilRX, we're offering you, our valued customer, a special opportunity to upgrade to AmoxicilRX 2.0 Pro for only $29.95. Visit our web site for details.

Once again, thank you for upgrading, and welcome to the relativelyef-fectivesecuretechnologies.com family. And remember, family is forever!

Best Regards,
Raymond Bouchard, President
RelativelyEffectiveSecureTechologies, Inc.

MILESTONES IN THE HISTORY OF COMPUTING

"A refusal is not the act of a friend:"
The Corleone Family introduces the Yes/Yes prompt

Johnny Fontane was a well-known S/360 guru. In the mid-seventies, he published several technical articles and was renown for his programming prowess. However, in later years, he stopped honing his skills, and three operating systems later, Johnny was a has-been. No one would hire him.

An exciting DOS to ESA project involving a new LU6.2 application was being undertaken at one of the major studios. This conversion was heralded as one of the largest and most significant in the industry. Soon I.S. end-users at the studio would have their own PC workstations networked to a host application on the mainframe. It was a leading-edge application. This project was perfect for Johnny and would put him right back on top.

There was a problem. The CIO of the studio, a guy named Woltz, Jack Woltz, had it in for Johnny. Years earlier, when Fontane worked as a PAII for Woltz, he quit just before the rollout of a new database system. The project was delayed for months, and it weighed heavy on Woltz's performance review. "He made me look ridiculous," Woltz said. "And a man in my position can't afford to look ridiculous!" Woltz swore Johnny was washed-up in the industry.

Johnny had no choice but to turn to his Godfather, Don Corleone, a man not without influence in the industry himself.

Don knew how to handle these I.T. *pezzonovantes*. Years prior, Johnny worked as a contractor for an aerospace company and was presented with a fantastic offer from a competing company, but the project leader refused to release Johnny from his three-year contract.

Don and his friend, Lou Cabrasi, visited the project leader in the bursting room of his organization and made him an offer he couldn't refuse. Lou held the man near the paper shredder and Don assured him that either the contract or his *strutz* would be fed into it.

When a representative of Corleone's asked Woltz to grant this favor and give Johnny his second chance, Woltz became belligerent. "Never," he said. "Johnny never gets that job. And just in case Corleone tries any rough stuff, you tell him, I ain't no project leader. Yeah, I heard that story."

Woltz had a weakness, though. He was a PC nut and was especially proud of his new 500-gig hard disk and loved to show it off.

One morning, soon after Corleone's representative had arrived back in New York to personally deliver his response, Woltz woke up next to his disk drive's read/write head, and the very next day, Johnny got the job.

All the news that's fit to feed

Two tin cans and string push 33.6 bps

What started as an employee perk for working parents two years ago has developed into literally the next generation of computer engineers.

"We monitored a group of toddlers," David Haiku, director of interns at the XEROX PARC day-care center, said. "Two in particular worked with Tinker Toys until they created what looked an awful lot like the Copley DX103e, technology we had been developing for four years. Their model resolved a fundamental vortex relation issue we thought intractable."

The matrix the youngsters devised went from "playroom to lab" with only a brief stop to wipe the grape jelly from the structure. "It was the children's ability to develop without established boundaries which drove us to fund this lab. Now, we aggressively recruit and hire students right out of school."

One prodigy, Zach Hoya, was the object of a heated recruitment battle. "When he graduated from the Stamford Nursery School," Haiku said, "labs from all over tried to woo him, touching off a bidding war. Hoya, who just wanted to play blocks with his friend Josh, was finally won over when the kitty was sweetened with a Recaro toddler car seat and a kite."

Hoya joined a top gun team including Research Triangle Park Kindergarten wonder boys, Cody and Jason Sears, and the MIT Experimental School for Gifted Fingerpainters' Becky Hunter.

The team's first product was a faster abacus processor. "The tykes lubricated the wires with the strawberry filling from a Pop-Tart and achieved 50 percent faster calculations with less heat generation."

Power naps are credited for much of the creativity. Last Thursday, after awakening fresh and rejuvenated, Hoya and the Sears boys managed to push 33.6 bps through two tin cans and some string.

But does all play and no work make Chuckie a dull boy? "They have their moments," Haiku said. "A little precocious mischief is healthy relief and can even be constructive. For example, just yesterday, they wrote their first virus."

Apparently, Zach and Cody had "infected" a few sheets of the carbon paper used in the lab. Every copy that comes out now bears their political view that "Becky's got cooties."

Reflections on the Y2K crisis:

Those organizations that wholesale converted all dates to four-digits were left with either unnecessary work or a short-sighted solution. For example, does a carton of milk really require a four-digit year for expiration? At the other extreme, is a four-digit year enough for a can of SPAM?

If your hard drive looks anything like your basement, it's time to check-in

Hello. My name is Chris, and I'm a PC pack rat.

For as long as I can remember, I've collected PC files. I never deleted anything. As I accumulated more and more, my 120-meg hard drive would no longer do. I graduated to a 320, then to a 1-gig drive. It would seem that nothing could satisfy my hard drive requirements. But then, in the spring of 1996, my whole PC world collapsed when my company relocated me.

When we moved, we took with us only those few things that would fit in our car. The other 29,410 pounds of our stuff went into storage where it's being safely stored since. (At least we trust it's safely stored—my wife claims she saw some of her hand-made quilts at a recent swap meet.)

With little surplus space, my desktop computer didn't make the cut. Instead, I crammed my old notebook computer with its 80-meg HD under the passenger seat. In its day, that notebook was quite a machine. Its day was July 16th, 1987. Today, it's not much, but it would have to suffice for the three months (which has now turned into six months) it would take to complete our new home.

Fast forward to yesterday: my wife and I, relaxing in our temporary housing, were discussing how surprisingly little we missed our "stuff" in storage. She was talking about furniture, clothes and other items. I was talking about my hard drive.

In that one moment, I realized I had kicked my megabyte habit. I had gone five months without the stuff that I had spent years accumulating, and I survived. Survived! And you can too.

Now, I can't recommend my cold turkey method for everyone. So instead, I've developed a 7-step recovery program. Follow this simple plan and you'll never have to upgrade again:

1. Self-assessment

List the files on your hard drive with a cataloging utility. If you're like me, one of the first things you'll notice is that you have five different cataloging utilities. Review your files with a spouse or significant other—make a night of it. As a litmus test, try to justify everything you have. If you find yourself not very convincing, you have some candidates for the trash can icon. My wife called me to task on a 61-meg folder containing GIFs from the *Mod Squad*, Quick-Time movie clips from box-office flops, and sound files from *Marcel Marceau Live at the Met*.

2. Journal your progress

When you make this first pass at banishing files to Cyberia, you're likely to be a little overzealous. Use one of the nine shareware text editors you've been evaluating for eighteen months to keep track of all you've deleted and where you got it or how you can recreate it. This way, when you delete something that might come in handy later, oh, say, OS2.INI (Windows and Macintosh users substitute the critical file of your choice), you're not up the proverbial creek.

3. Eliminate the slack

It's bad enough that you have so many unnecessary files, but do they have to take up so much space? No. Compact all your candidate files into an archive using one of the twelve compression utilities you've amassed. You may have just reclaimed up to 50 percent of your hard drive, but don't stop now ...

4. Offload that excess baggage

Your files have been ZIPed or STUFFed and you don't miss them. Offload those compressed files from Step 3 onto some of those junk diskettes you've stockpiled. You know, the ones with the half-scraped-off labels you've saved from demos and old program installs that you knew would come in handy some day. Well, you're vindicated. This is that day and, yes, you can even use 5¼ diskettes for this task as long as you blow the dust off them first—you don't want that antique floppy drive to experience any read errors, do you?

5. Take that big step

As a symbolic as well as purposeful milestone, throw away the archive diskettes. This has two benefits: it forever frees hard drive space and it gets rid of those diskettes you've saved—they really never were worth saving; I was just kidding in Step 4, but now you accept this as the truth.

6. Evaluation

Pat yourself on the back or kick yourself in the behind based on your response to the following questions you pose to yourself:

1. Did I delete the original files from my hard drive after I created the archive? Yes (pat) or No (kick).
2. Did I delete the archives from my hard drive after I copied them to diskette? Yes (pat) or No (kick).
3. Did I run some sort of undelete program to recover everything I deleted because I was afraid to "take that leap?" Yes (kick), No (pat), or "Hmmm, I didn't think of that." (kick).

7. Maintenance

Repeat Steps 1 - 6 every month. Ahh, you thought you were home free, but you have a pathological problem which requires maintenance. Like a weight problem, you don't just diet once; you diet for life.

There ought to be a line of greeting cards just for us.
For instance:

> **Outside of card:** Sorry to hear you've been outsourced ...
> **Inside of card:** Be sure to upload that virus before they revoke your user ID.

> **Outside of card:** Good luck at your new job ...
> **Inside of card:** Call me if there are any other opportunities there!

> **Outside of card:** Congratulations on your promotion ...
> **Inside of card:** But before you go, would you like to take this knife out of my back? You'll probably need it again.

Jokes they might tell if the big names played the main room at COMDEX ...

Dennis Miller: "I'm not sure how anyone could believe Al Gore invented the Internet. I mean, the other day someone asked him to define *DOS* and he said it was the number two in Spanish."

Henny Youngman: "Took my kid for a walk, he says, 'Dad, what's SDRAM?' I say, 'I dunno.' He says, 'What's a triggered interrupt?' I say, 'I dunno.' He says, 'What's overclocking?' I say, 'I dunno.' He says, 'Sorry to keep asking questions.' I say, 'That's OK, how do you expect to learn?'"

Johnny Carson, as *Carnac the Magnificent*: "May the bugs of many programs infest your bin directory."

Bob Hope: "I just got a new PC; PC, that stands for 'piece of crap.'"

Jay Leno: "I don't want to say our data center manager has smelly feet, but he took his shoes off and the Halon dropped! Rim shot! Hey, is this mike on mute?"

Steve Allen: "I just got a gigabyte. And if you've ever had your *giga* bitten, you know exactly how painful that is."

David Brenner: "Boy, we got bad response time in my shop. I mean, we don't measure it in milliseconds, we measure it in *Mississippis*. You press ENTER and go, 'one-Mississippi, two-Mississippi ...'"

George Burns: "Gracie, define *modem*."
Gracie Allen: "It's what gardeners do to lawns."

Yakov Smirnoff: "Wadda country. Here, popular programs are *PageMaker*, *Klondike*, and *Excel*. In my country, we have *Leisure Suit Leonid the Party Animal, Ready, Set, Where Are You Going?* and the most popular program in Russia: *Waiting in line for toilet paper*."

Rodney Dangerfield: "No respect at all. I bought a Las Vegas simulator. I loosened my tie and slipped $50 in the disk drive. It shut down on me."

Robin Williams: "Virtual storage, what a concept."

Freddie Prinze: "The data center called because one of the initiators was spiking at, like, 90 percent, and I said, 'Hey, it's not my *yob*.'"

Andy Kaufman's *foreign man*: "I don't know if you're laughing with me, at me, or if your beepers are on vibrate and you're being paged! But *tank you vedy much*."

Rich Little: "'Cheeeeeeesh—bing-bong—bing-bong' ... that was the sound of a 28.8 modem connecting. Here's another one you might recognize, 'You've got mail!' Thanks. I'm here all week."

Bill Maher: Why do I look so scared? George W. Bush has his finger on the button and this guy doesn't know his ASCII from a hole in the ground. I mean, I honestly believe that his idea of Intellectual Property is Stephen Hawking's Cambridge townhouse."

Jack Benny: "I *am* 39 years old. Hex 39."

Jerry Seinfeld (addressing a heckler): "Hey buddy, I don't come to where you work and tell you how to empty the shredder bin!"

Chestnuts roasting on an open fire and other OSHA violations

Ctrl-Alt-Delete those holiday trinkets

I don't know what it is about us computer types. During the holidays, I have a painted-on smile that's bigger than Bozo the Clown's. Each of my relatives finds a different computer trifle to give me, and I have to act appreciative.

``Mom, thanks. What is it?''

``It's a walnut with eyes, sitting next to a computer terminal. Computer nut. Get it? Cute, huh?''

You know, I really do feel sorry for that Powatamee tribe if this is the best they can do.

``Aunt Lois, where did you ever find an ergonomic mouse soap-on-a-rope?''

``Do you like it, Chris? I mean, if you don't, I saved the receipt.''

``No, it's great. It'll, uh, come in handy.'' Yeah, like when I'm looking for something to hang myself with.

``Uncle Don, you didn't have to.''

``Well, I know you work with computers, and I thought you'd get a kick out of it. It's a chocolate computer diskette. High density.''

``Terrific. Now I can really put that new version of Norton Utilities through its paces.''

``I'm really embarrassed, cousin Peter. I didn't get you anything and ... and ... you got me this most excellent ... this tasty-looking ...

fruitcake in the shape of a hand scanner.''

``Well, I remember how your eyes lit up last year when your brother got the cheese log in the shape of a Nintendo Power Glove, so I shopped and shopped, and I finally found this for you.''

``What a lucky break for me that you did!''

``You didn't think your grandmother would forget you, did you? I know you have a computer at home so I got you this little magnet to stick on it.''

``It says, `I♥Computers.' Gee, and all I got you were these fuzzy dice to hang from your walker. Gram, I'll think of you every time I have to degauss my monitor.''

What I really want to know is where people even find junk like this and why the local authorities haven't placed some sort of embargo on its trade.

I'd like to give an award for the most inane computer gift. Maybe the award should be some type of self-detonating device.

The reason I'm so out of the holiday spirit is that there are so many good gifts out there for us computer nuts.

Call me radical, but I would prefer to receive a nice sweater rather than a box of blank floppy disks any day. (Or simply give me the gift that keeps on giving: an annuity.) But you can't tell friends and relatives that.

``What? More? Ahh, you guys are just too generous.''

``We know what a wine connoisseur you are. So, naturally, when we saw this in the store ...''

``Cold duck in a Herman Hollerith decanter? You shouldn't have. And I am really serious. You really shouldn't have.''

Seen on a desktop in a SYSPROG's cubicle:

> "My manager went to COMDEX and all I got was this lousy mouse pad!"

The other salary survey

The response to last month's annual survey was so overwhelming that not all categories of respondents could be appropriately represented. This supplement reports not on the conventional categories of manufacturing, service, or government sectors, but on a class of IS professional traditionally under-represented on salary surveys: the underground industries.

Fully 18% of you reported providing IS services to some illegal activity which we've broken down into four new categories: theft rings (smugglers, art thieves, or poachers), organized crime (international cartels, domestic syndicates, or independent strong arms), political *persona non grata* (CIA covert operations, Sandinistas, terrorists, or arms dealers), and miscellaneous underground economies like swap meet dealers and shareware authors.

Their responsibilities

In general, our delinquent DP colleagues have responsibilities and qualifications similar to ours. Mahat Sareilei, an AIX client-server architect for a tortoise smuggling ring based near the Philippines, has an MS from MIT. "I can make a bundle in the 'real world,'" Sareilei said, "but this is a family business, and we enjoy working for ourselves."

Working in the IS wing of other family businesses, though, isn't always as personally rewarding. Sonny Bustamente is the IS director for the "Barzini Family" business. "If I could, I would leave," Bustamente said, "but I can't. I would lose my insurance benefits."

Bustamente is like many others in his field, a prisoner in golden handcuffs. "I work sixteen-hour days doing the work of five on outdated hardware," Carlito Javare, Production Support Analyst for a Central American guerrilla army, said. "Sometimes, when I process the day's transactions of government payoffs, I wonder if this is the job for me. But then I get my weekly stipend of $8000 cash and I say, 'Si!'"

What do they know

Javare's situation is typical of the darker side of an industry where mainframe leases and traditional product support contracts are harder to initiate; and where, in general, their technology lags behind their legitimate counterparts. It's no surprise then that their familiarity in what we take for granted is lacking: only 18% were familiar with Windows XP while 59.7% were familiar with 3.1 and a staggering 81.9% were familiar with the local appeal process.

Their compensation

So how *are* the dirt bags of our industry faring? By the results of our survey, pretty good (refer to figures 1 and 2). Underground IS management positions averaged $600,000 per year in tax-free income. The staff reaped a respectable average of $225,000 per year. This is up 20% because of a sagging dollar. Raises in general, though,

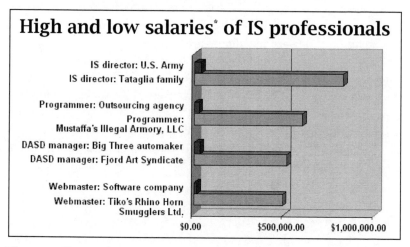

Figure 1. *Base salary plus benefits. All amounts in US dollars.

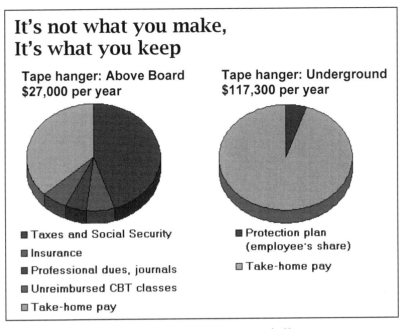

It's not what you make, It's what you keep

Tape hanger: Above Board
$27,000 per year

Tape hanger: Underground
$117,300 per year

- Taxes and Social Security
- Insurance
- Professional dues, journals
- Unreimbursed CBT classes
- Take-home pay

- Protection plan (employee's share)
- Take-home pay

Figure 2. What you take home matters most of all.

are flat. "I have not seen one in two years," says Françios Chevalier, network administrator for the French digital signature forgery ring known as *Clockwork L'Orange*, "but your weak currency spells more discretionary income for those in our field."

Indeed, when not adjusted for the exchange rate, few of our purloining peers saw an increase. Instead, they're being wooed with a variety of non-cash benefits including flex-time, telecommuting, and offsites to extravagant locations. Last spring, for example, Fazel Shramak gave his team a break from writing viruses for the government and set out to develop an *esprit de corp*. "We set them loose on the target side of an Iranian firing range with only a slingshot and someone else's eye-glasses," Shramak said. "It was a win-win situation for me. I sold it to the staff as a team-building exercise, and I sold it to my management as a head-count reduction thing."

New responsibilities

Like many of us, the brigands experienced increased responsibility this past year. Too, it rarely translated into increased compensation in an industry where things like mergers and acquisitions are taken in stride. When the Cali Cartel went to war with the Medellin Cartel, the resulting hostile takeover of territory spelled what Medellin Help desk manager Marta Laling called "execution-style downsizing." That Marta survived the merger and was even promoted to director shows how serious the cartels are to recognize the abilities of women. "There's no glass ceiling here," Laling said. "Many women have senior positions in cartel back offices." To be sure, our survey shows the gender gap in the cartels is narrowing. Salaries of women are right up there with their male counterparts. "This is a stark contrast to the syndicates in this country," Robert Gastoff, organized crime technology trends analyst for Popular Cryptography magazine, said. "Here, if a wiseguy is indicted, the employer provides for the worker's family. In the cartels, though, if a man is locked-up, his old lady is expected to pick-up the slack."

The future forecast

If the FBI crime statistics are any measure, the future looks pretty good for the reprobates of our industry. "But expect change," Gastoff says. "I see the most growth in the networking technologies. One word: Internet." Gastoff said the cartels, rings, and other illicit operations have been talking about merging for some time to cut expenses, but they've lacked a technical strategy for tying all their applications together. The Internet, he says, provides a cost-effective method for reducing operating expenses while bringing in new technology and providing improved service levels for their end users.

"If I were an underground IS professional," Gastoff said, "I would be honing my IP skills. Oh, and I would watch my back. That's always good advice."

Soft skills

Don't say "maybe" unless you mean it

A CEO can go only so far with a knowledge of IT trends and technology. To be truly effective, the executive must excel in the interpersonal disciplines. Your must be able to motivate, communicate, and negotiate.

Forget about your Y2K problems, reorganizations, and service levels few minutes and focus on improving your "soft skills."

Motivating the staff

Have you ever asked yourself, "Why do *I* always get the disgruntled employees?" Maybe you need to stop and take an arm's reach look at your org chart. Impersonal vertical organizations are fast going the way of vacuum-tubes as are the Darth Vader 'my way or the highway' management techniques. They simply don't work. Your staff needs to be motivated, not intimidated.

Vulgar incentives like money, high-end workstations, or a well-appointed cubicle are not motivators, by the way. Your staff can get those from a competitor. Give them something they don't get anywhere else like respect, a feeling of importance, and a sense of having a positive impact on the organization. In short, engage your staff by allowing them a part in the decision-making process.

You're probably saying, "Get the 'H' out of here! My staff? C'mon, these are the same people who wear sandals and Bermuda shorts to work in February. Pamper, coddle, and cajole, sure. But empower? As Dana Carvey doing President Bush would say, 'Not gonna do it, wouldn't be prudent.'"

Well, you have to do it. But remember, their decision skills are still in the budding phase, you need to "direct" their choices to both give them the support they need and get the end result you want. How?

If you want a five year-old to wear a long-sleeved shirt, you don't tell him to wear one. He'll revolt; no one likes to be told what to do. Instead, you ask if they want to wear the Snoopy long sleeved shirt or the Spiderman long-sleeved shirt.

Want your people to bring in a project by 3Q when all indicators suggest a more realistic date is six months later? Ask them which target makes more sense: July 1 or September 30. They'll recommend the later date, of course, but now they're engaged. And committed.

Sinister? Maybe. But certainly effective, and that's why your cube has the mahogany veneer trim.

Working with vendors

So you read "The Art of the Deal" and wrangled a '77 Ford Grenada hubcap for half of what the guy at the swap meet was originally asking. Now you think you're ready to negotiate an outsourcing contract? Here's a news flash. The "love it or shove it" Tony Soprano approach simply doesn't play in corporate negotiations.

If the going rate for outsourcing is $2.25 per line of code and you hold steadfast at $1.49, you can expect to get the equivalent of either a factory second—defective code written by cheap inexperienced labor—or worse, a racked-up invoice because the consultants have "determined" subroutines and code reuse are "not appropriate" for your project.

Indeed, nowhere is the adage "you get what you pay for" more true than with vendors.

But whether they're service agreements or hardware leases, you should know the other downside to playing hardball with sales people: you can kiss the leather mouse pad and the high-tech thermo-aluminum coffee mug "incentives" goodbye.

Reporting to superiors

Is dealing with senior management an unnerving experience?

Here's a thought: the Peter Principle says each person rises to the level of their own incompetence and, well, you just can't rise any higher than CEO. So do the math.

Wipe that smile off your face. Actually, most CEOs are *not* incompetent, but it's easy to see how an IT executive might get the wrong impression. Because you must distill complex issues into one-page briefs or digest months of research into a handful of presentation foils, your might think your boss is incapable of grasping the complexity of your organization. They can, of course, but that's not their job, it's yours.

As bottom line people, they don't need to wade through your data. For them, you simply roll-up your conclusions. Oh, and make sure they are good ones because contrary to what you might have heard on the audio version of *The Portable MBA*, it *is* allowable to shoot the messenger.

So then, how do you make bad news sound good? It's actually pretty easy. In your update, just replace negative "struggling words" with positive ones. For instance, you don't make headway, you progress; and you don't spend, you invest. Also, liberally pepper your status report with proven performance words like "facilitate," "benefit," and "accomplish." Here are a few examples:

- Completion is deferred to facilitate the inclusion of base functions. (The project is late.)
- We've found it beneficial to invest additional funds in order to secure a positive ROI. (It's over budget.)
- We've accomplished functioning outside the constraints of adhering to the original objectives. (And it still doesn't work right.)

Succinct remarks on your presentation are to be expected: "Outstanding. Stellar performance, Mitchell. Keep up the good work." Be sure and say "thank you" as your gather your foils. And try and keep a straight face.

Sticky Situations

Delicate personnel issues, not technical ones, give an executive the most grief. Test your soft skills and see how well you can think on your feet by taking this quiz. There is no one right answer, and there is no scoring, but feel free to run anything you're unclear about by HR.

You've spent weeks preparing a board presentation. Two minutes before you're scheduled to deliver it, you notice your admin assistant copied the foils 2-sided because "it was the green thing to do." Do you ...

a)   ... secretly hook the overhead cord around the nearest chair and ask the person sitting in it to scoot over a bit, knocking the overhead to the ground?

b)   ... accept the blame saying, "It's my fault for hiring her."

True or False: "I make the rules, I break the rules" is an appropriate response when your webmaster asks if "www.wine-aficionado.com" complies with your organization's web browsing policy.

At the company picnic, your staff is trying to talk you into riding the rented mechanical bull. You ...

a)   ... graciously pass because your "building bridges, not walls" mediation skills are needed at a brooding argument between the engineers over the appropriate formation of charcoal briquettes for the best heat dissipation.

b)   ... laugh and reluctantly acquiesce, but on Monday transfer them to the shipping department.

Complete this sentence: If you need to learn about business ethics ...

a)   ... you have to buy two separate books.

b)   ... you're not ready for IT management.

At an all-hands meeting, your newest project manager mentions he is selling Girl Scout cookies for his daughter's troop. You ...

a)   ... tell him to "put everyone in the room down for a dozen."

b)   ... threaten to report this egregious violation of corporate policy to security unless he pays you a "tribute" of two boxes of the minty ones.

The Kotter Model

Named for the Brooklyn high school instructor, Gabe Kotter, the Kotter Model merges qualified instructors and students in a productive learning organization. Knowledge is transferred, work gets done. It's a wonderful environment not just to work in, but to take credit for, as well. Everyone wins.

Best of all, it's simple to implement: just combine the best attributes of pre-, grade-, high-, and post-secondary schools into your organization in a way that facilitates learning as well as productivity.

For example, one of the most common Kotter Model devices adopted is the "Work Day Partition." The Work Day Partition, or simply WDP, divides the work day, 8:00 - 3:50, into eight 50-minute periods. A 110-decibel blow horn sees to it that there is no task spill-over between periods which means, for instance, that no staff meeting can go more than fifty minutes. Water-cooler chit-chat, personal phone calls, and web-surfing are effectively contained in the seven 10-minute slack times between periods. You gain staff productivity without infringing on their ability to run a cottage business from the office. Are you beginning to see the benefits of the Kotter Model?

Here are a few other practices expressed in the model:

Team redefined

The team concept is *passé*. Tasks are, instead, meted-out to project "fraternities." A project fraternity consists of senior staff and "pledges." Pledges go through an initiation or hazing rite to create a special bond of trust with fellow workers. Hazing may be as benign as insisting the "plebe" wear a suit and tie for an entire week (software developers find this particularly challenging) or worse: forcing their participation in cruel drinking games like the notorious "drink week-old cold coffee until you chuck." Project fraternities are natural time managers, as well, who can accomplish an entire quarter's work in one all-nighter—the result of which is a higher quality of life for them. Reward them with t-shirts emblazoned with Greek-sounding names like "Gamma-Lambda-Enigma-Pajama" or "Telly Savalas."

Corporal punishment

If you've ever thought, "What Novak needs is a good kick in the ..." Ahhh, on second though, maybe you better not.

Nap time

1990's "results-oriented" conditioning has taught us that sleeping on the job is an egregious violation of the work ethic. But how many times have you come back from an afternoon employee-farewell gathering or a seminar buffet lunch only to spend the remainder of the day walking to your slot in the mail room every five minutes to keep awake? Kotter calls the time after lunch the "productivity regeneration" period. Get out your sleeping roll, take a power nap, then get back to work. But don't forget to set your alarm, or you'll have to cut and paste "I will not oversleep" 500 times on your weekly status report.

Report cards

Annual performance reviews are much too nebulous to be of any benefit either for employee development or as evidence in an unlawful termination suit. To that end, the Kotter Model does away with performance reviews and introduces, in their place, report cards. Staff can now be "graded" A-F on several specific tasks like reading (company memorandum comprehension), 'riting (status reports are turned-in by 1:00 P.M. Friday), and 'rithmetic (expense report amounts are appropriately subtotaled where indicated). The Model also permits job-specific write-in criteria like hygiene and "getting along with others."

Prayer

The Kotter Model suggests you begin each work day with a prayer. A way to avert the potential controversy associated with introducing spirituality into the workplace is to instead include the deity of preference in your company's mission statement, e.g., "We will be a profitable organization if it be the will of Zeus" or "Like the sacred Phoenix worshipped by the Phoenicians, we will rise from Chapter 11." Mission statements like these can even be included in your company's annual report or 10-K—which no one looks at too closely—though you may want to leave them out of your prospectus.

While Kotter defines many other effective processes, you should remember it is an "open model." Be innovative yourself. Incorporate those methods into your organization which most facilitated the learning process in your own education.

Three things techies do with their beepers

1. Turn them on vibrator mode and have beeper races on the conference room table with colleagues.

2. Beep a co-worker with a bogus number (local bowling alley, gentleman's club, or anything in Malaysia) just about the time they've merged into the evening freeway rush-hour melee.

3. Turn them off to conserve energy.

All the news that's fit to feed

Three-million-dollar man introduced

"RISC technology, client-server architecture, and a catastrophic jet-ski accident" was how government researcher Dr. Rudy Wells of the OSI explained the origins of his new three-million-dollar man. "It's twenty-five years later," he said yesterday, referring to his original breakthrough in bionic engineering, "and we've developed faster, cheaper, and more powerful cyborg technology."

Wells previewed his bionic man, code named "Leo," at last week's Technomedical Conference in Austin where innovators meet annually to discuss the year's advancements in organ and limb regeneration. OSI spokesman Oscar Goldman indicated Leo would be profiled in-depth in next month's *New England Journal of Bionics* where previous showcases included Andrew Wysocki's hernia emulator and Russell Merrik's nonpreemptive spastic colon (currently in beta test).

Goldman explained that this is not your father's bionic man. "Where we began with an eye, arm, and legs ... today we've automated the brain and circulatory system as well. We're also exploiting new technology. For example," he said, "in 1974, our man could run as fast as a Ford Maverick in third gear, or he could squeeze a coconut open with his right arm. But he couldn't do both at the same time. Today, thanks to distributed processing and multitasking, he can."

"Leo is amazing," Wells added. "His eyes have 3600 DPI resolution and OCR software that enable him to actually read; his central nervous system is controlled by a processor so fast it can perform an infinite loop in two seconds and so powerful it requires two halt instructions to stop it.

"If that's not enough, Leo has an eleventh toe that accepts an RG59 cable—he's got a built-in Internet backbone connection."

Oracle announces $500 man

Commenting that the average household doesn't need the power and sophistication of a top-of-the-line bionic man, Oracle Corp.'s Larry Ellison announced that his company has defined standards for the creation of a $500 man. Ellison's vision of a pseudo-intelligent humanoid companion is economically plausible, he said, because of two factors: "SIMM dumping and a surplus of mannequin limbs in Brazil."

Oracle is offering several upgrades to their "common man" including a hard drive in the event you expect him to remember anything. "The base model doesn't do much," Ellison said, "but what do you expect for $500, Albert Schweitzer?"

Pat, I'd like to buy a vowel

When did good old-fashioned business become "e-Business?" Likely it was sometime after dead-ends became *cul-de-sacs* and before stuff even the Salvation Army wouldn't take for artillery practice became the fashionable "distressed look."

Since that time, though, retailing has become "e-tailing," soft-copy tomes have become "e-Books," pinging a site is "e-vailability monitoring," and password validation is "e-security."

Is this an indication of exciting new technology or just an Earl Scheib paint job on a '78 Chevy Monte Carlo?

Denise Radke, who runs her successful "iSecond that Promotion" marketing group out of Menlo Park, California, with husband Mitch, suggests it's the latter. "It comes down to what *sounds* leading edge ... new."

"Grammatically speaking, consonants are passive and vowels are active," says Mitch Radke. "All the better that 'i' exemplifies Internet or individualism, and 'e' reeks of excellence or, at the very least, electronic. From a marketing perspective, those letters are a lot easier to sell than the unfortunate acronym representing a 'brick and mortar' business."

Yet, with successful "e-i" vowel appendages—eBay, iMac, e*Trade, iBook, eMachine, and the AS/400e—one has to ask what the chances are for break-outs like A, O, and U.

"No doubt, we would like to exploit the other vowels," Denise says, "but our research shows that 'i' works well for consumer products and services; and, with the exception of that *E. Coli* thing, 'e' has been embraced by everyone from B2B industries to retail shoppers."

eVerything old is new again

To what origin can we attribute this marketing *coup d'état*?

Polaroid's new i-Zone "sticker film" camera? C'mon, that just came out and may not even be around by the time you read this.

Steve Jobs' NeXT computer? No, e-mail was around before that.

Issac Asimov's seminal 1950 book, *I, Robot* or the ubiquitous IHOP? Doubtful.

"Actually, vowelization has been practiced for years," Denise says. "The i-beam, of course, made modern skyscrapers possible; and for almost three decades, Disneyland named its premier attractions (Space Mountain, Matterhorn Bobsleds, Pirates of the Caribbean, etc...) 'E ticket' rides. But if you had to trace the phenomenon you would be hard-pressed to go further back than *I Ching*, the ancient Chinese book of changes," she says.

More to the point, the latest wave of vowelization continues the tradition of breathing new life into matured technology, products, and services. For instance, consider the following:

- When Shreveport, Louisana-based, National Prison Suppliers renamed its LoJack-type prisoner monitoring ankle cuff to "iCon," sales increased 160 percent.

- Online optometry supplier, "See the Difference," renamed its classic paper Snellen "P E Z O L C F T D" poster "the iChart," and the yellowed placards flew off the shelf.

- Before renaming their band "iRon Butterfly," the boomer rockers couldn't give away MP3s of their "In-A-Gadda-Da-Vida." Now they can. (With downloads rumored to be in the double-digits, there may be hope, still, for eNgland Dan and John Ford Coley.)

- At Wally's Best Autos, in Fort Wayne, Indiana, owner Jimmy Correa was beginning to wonder whether buying a wholesale fleet of 1990 Yugos was such a wise decision after all. But taking a hint from both the prominent Mercedes E Class and the BMW 'i' series, Correa renamed his "fine pre-owned automobiles" the Yugo "i" series. "Inside of a week," Correa says, "the happy new owners had them all towed off our lot."

Coming full circle—right down the toilet

So what's it all mean? A renaissance for e. e. cummings? "Brady Bunch"-like syndication success for "iDream of Jeannie?" Actually, more like a downward spiral. What happens when everyone picks a kitchy name for products and services? It causes industry confusion, begging the question, "Is this a core business or a fad?" Put more simply, the e's and i's are simply overused. iCarumba, e-nuff already!

Lest we forget ...

Yes, the industry has been diagnosed with a vowel-obstruction problem—the vowel is obstructing the real core product or service. Still, there is no sign of remission.

What's more troubling than the overuse of vowels is the bias against the Rodney-Dangerfield-of-vowels—the "sometimes Y." We have already determined we cannot beat them. So if we're going to join them, we may as well have equal representation. To that end, and in deference to the oft-ignored Y, here are some new vowel-enhanced terms to add to our lexicon:

y-businesses are college counseling services. They direct students away from MBA programs and toward advanced degrees in liberal arts where they'll have the broad background to ask the questions that have piqued philosophers through the ages like, "would you like that super-sized?"

yWitnessNews is anonymous streamed videos of news as it happens, captured and broadcast by people who "don't want to get involved."

Y*Trade is one of a new breed of brokerage firms that permit traders to neither buy nor sell stock. "Our philosophy is that any commission is bad," a Y*Trade representative said. "Paying $7 to buy or sell, for example, is 700 shares of a penny stock you could own." Y*Trade has yet to develop a business model and appears to have no chance of ever turning a profit. But that hasn't stopped three top Wall Street firms from courting its IPO.

yMac is new line of desktop workstations that asks, "With all those great viruses available on our Wintel platforms, why would you want a Macintosh?"

Don't quote me

"First I discover America.

But I never understood this 'Horse With No Name' they sang of.

So I dropped them.

Then I devote my time to discovering some other act that can make me big money.

Next thing I know, I'm running a contracting business."

—Christopher Columbus
on the discovery of the consultant, 1505.

Randy Mikado: unplugged!

Has wireless technology delivered on its promise? Oh, and by the way, what was the promise of wireless technology?

Found 1980s correspondence reveals the original vision.

Wireless technology. It's what everyone seems to be talking about. At this year's COMDEX, for instance, attendance at eMobility sessions was second only to attendance at the Riviera's "Crazy Girls" revue.

But is wireless technology pushing a new envelope or licking an old one? It's not new, of course. We've had pagers and cell phones for almost two decades.

What *is* new are wireless applications in IT. But many vendors, buoyed only by the hype of its immense potential, are struggling for a defined position in a still undefined market.

As R&D labs and CIOs alike wrestle with this alleged potential, they are left wondering if wireless technology can ever come to fruition without a clear set of standards. In short, the fundamental question—"What good is wireless?"—has largely been left unanswered.

Will we be liberated by mobility or be enslaved to battery capacity, cell tower availability, and hemorrhaging security exposures? How can we know? No one has ever defined the promise of wireless technology.

Well, actually, someone has.

In 1984, when personal computers and cell phones were in their respective forests primeval, the now defunct Zeta-80 Institute—a think tank sponsored by Atari, Coleco, and Commodore—studied the potential of wireless technology. While the complete study is unavailable (the original tapes are unreadable on any of today's devices), one interoffice memo thread between researcher Randy Mikado and his project manager, Owen Sidmann, survives. Mikado, widely regarded as the father of wireless applications, outlined his vision of the technology's potential in these memos. Though never realized in his lifetime (tragically, in 1991, he died when a vending machine he was violently shaking fell on him), Mikado's proposals may help you position wireless technology in your enterprise now, nearly twenty years later.

What follows are the memos that passed between the two men during those early days when wireless communication was merely one more agenda item on the think tank's list of brainstorming topics.

March 15, 1984
TO: Owen Sidmann
FROM: Randy Mikado

Owen, I've completed A42210 and G15038; the reports are attached. Let's talk about my next project. As I mentioned at the Christmas Party (by the way, didn't you think the one-legged tap-dancer was a treat) I would like to transition into the medical research group. I have some ideas for developing artificial kidney stones and grafting acne. Did you know there has been a lot of progress in Romania growing appendixes in baboons? That there is incredible opportunity in this area I can say with the same assuredness as I believe "One Day at a Time" will join "I Love Lucy" in perpetual reruns.

March 16, 1984
TO: Randy
FROM: Owen Sidmann

Were you paying attention at Monday's staff meeting? You're working the wireless project. The report's due April 13. By the way, you need to rework your conclusions in the A42210 and G15038 reports when you get a chance. The description of your device that permits you to see through walls six inches thick sounds a lot like a window, and Dick has summarily rejected your proposal for a parachute that opens on impact. Perhaps some type of air cushion or air bag would be more practical.

This is a think tank, Randy. Think! Have a nice weekend.

March 21, 1984
TO: Owen Sidmann
FROM: Randy Mikado

I was out of the office for the past two days—Joanne had chickenpox. I would have liked to see your note sooner, but I had no way to access office information from home or from the doctor's office where we sat waiting for hours. But I did have some time this morning to think about wireless; being detached for two days gave rise to an idea. What if we could leverage cell phone technology and somehow merge it with the technology that permits pagers to display phone numbers? We could have an *information appliance* that could retrieve information from the data center. With the advent of satellite technology pushing bits through the air like so many droplets of acid rain, the potential of such *e-mobility* is beyond imagination. I say that with the same assuredness that I believe *Jaws 3-D* will be bigger than *The Sound of Music.*

March 23, 1984
TO: Randy
FROM: Owen Sidmann

E-mobility. I like that. The scarcity of cell towers in urban areas, I suspect, will not be an issue as the devices become more popular. One concern, though—would such a device be useful on a plane where executives spend most of their time away from the office? And what about battery capacity? How useful would a device be if it fails at the least convenient time? The technology sounds promising, but one barrier might be the displacement of an existing access network. In other words, why would someone want wireless if they're already wired for an internal network or external modem access? I think the key is in the applications. Let Nigel's team take over the technology side. I want you to focus on applications. What applications do you envision? Remote database access? Inventory access?

March 27, 1984
TO: Owen Sidmann
FROM: Randy Mikado

Owen, sorry I missed you. Here's a draft of H85903.1. It is the first application, remote access, and is very exciting. I say that with the same assuredness that I believe Men at Work will be the next Beatles.

March 27, 1984
TO: Randy
FROM: Owen Sidmann

Randy, if I read your draft correctly, you are proposing a standard to remotely access data on a PC. That does, indeed, sound exciting. Though a lot of people see PCs as home hobby devices, I see a time when their power will rival the mainframe as we know it (though we are talking, perhaps, fifty years down the road) and be integrated into a data center. Unfortunately, I am not nearly as thrilled by your example. You say that people will be able to store music on a PC and access (i.e., listen to) that music from your new wireless appliance? If I am reading that correctly, I direct your attention to a document in our corporate library titled, "the encyclopedia." Such a device already exists. It was invented in 1895 by Guglielmo Marconi and is called "the radio." You'll have to do better than that.

March 27, 1984
TO: Owen Sidmann
FROM: Randy Mikado

I wanted to get something for you to read over the weekend, Owen. I've attached a very rough draft of H85903.2. It describes monitoring system performance and availability remotely via your cell phone. This is a great application of the technology. I say that with the same assuredness that I believe the Beta format will be the standard in home videotape technology.

March 30, 1984
TO: Randy
FROM: Owen Sidmann

I read your document over the weekend at a gas stop on our drive up to Gloucester (rained the whole time). Relying on a cell phone as the portal to your enterprise data is severely limiting in regards to the data you can garner. Plus, it could be downright irresponsible—I've heard of some municipalities discussing laws to prohibit cell phone use in moving vehicles. I mean, think about it. What would be the last thing you'd see while driving your K-car over a guard rail at fifty-five miles per hour? Your life passing before your eyes or the percentage of CPU in use by your server? Stay with it, Randy.

March 31, 1984
TO: Owen Sidmann
FROM: Randy

I see what you mean about the dangers of cell phone use. Perhaps we have pushed the technology as far as it can go. I mean, at six pounds, including the bag and antenna, how much smaller could they get? It's not like people will carry them in their vest pockets. However, I do believe there are some wireless commercial applications. H85903.3 outlines what I call mobility-commerce, or simply, "m-commerce." This is an application with unlimited potential. I say that with the same assuredness that I believe Tim Kazurinsky will be the next Lenny Bruce.

April 1, 1984
TO: Randy Mikado
FROM: Owen Sidmann

Randy, I am seriously thinking of shelving this project if this is the best you can come up with. Buying stuff over the phone is an exploitation of wireless technology? Well, look at me, I'm leading edge. I just ordered the three-album *Slim Whitman Anthology* over the phone. Does the phrase "operators are standing by" sound familiar? We can already buy things over the phone. Randy, I think you've reached an *impasse*, or worse, a dead end.

April 5, 1984
TO: Owen Sidmann
FROM: Randy

Let's agree that a mobile appliance would at least liberate staff from the constraints of hard-wired office access. In H85903.4, I've outlined how wireless applications can facilitate communication by making staff members available 24 hours a day/7 days a week using what I call interoffice electronic mail, or "IEmail." This electronic bridge is the future of successful office communication. I say that with same assuredness that I believe Ralph Macchio will be the next Brando.

April 10, 1984
TO: Randy
FROM: Owen Sidmann

Wireless correspondence. I can see it now. You're at your daughter's first piano recital. What? No metronome? What's that syncopating click you hear? Why, that's some nut in the back of the room who doesn't know when to stop working. Maybe grandpa wouldn't mind you multitasking—grieving and holding a meeting—at his wake, but the rest of the mourners do. Randy, one of our unwritten objectives is to advance technology without compromising the necessary balance people need in order to function. In other words, ankle transmitters might be appropriate for felons, but they are demoralizing when used to monitor staff on performance probation (B32219). Look, if you kick a mime long enough, you can make him talk, but that doesn't mean you've improved his communication. There is a soft side of communications I think you're missing in your aggressive pursuit of wireless applications. Take some time to stop and smell the roses, and I think you'll see there's more to life than staying connected to the office.

The thread abruptly ends there, no doubt just before Mikado has the opportunity to proclaim Laura Branigan the next Streisand. But the four-week dialog that transpired more than twenty years ago illustrates how both developers and users were just as polarized on the benefits and drawbacks of wireless technology as today's IT leaders are.

Whether you side with Mikado's relentless quest for a wireless application, which you know in your heart has a place in today's enterprise, or you share Mr. Sidmann's cynicism and believe you need to take a more cautious position, wireless technology has arrived and standards quickly need to be defined.

It may not happen overnight (in fact, it probably won't; "Melrose Place" is on tonight). But for now, at least, we have a couple of wireless applications: cell phones are great for making and receiving phone calls, and pagers are very effective at annoying people in theaters. That's a start.

Windows certification for executives

Don't even think about taking a certification exam before studying our sample test

Certification has typically been a way for people with liberal arts degrees to get jobs in the IT industry. But with technology changing faster than a Palm Pilot's batteries, CEOs are calling on you, their IT executive minions, to get certified. So you add yet another "to-do" item in your day-timer: "Take the certification exam." To help you ace it (it's almost impossible not to!), we've prepared this sample exam.

Windows Professional Certification Exam for Executives

You are about to take the certification exam for Windows professionals, developed especially for IT executives. Your success on this exam depends on a number of factors including your preparedness and resourcefulness.

General Instructions
1. Proceed only when the proctor instructs you to, unless you absolutely can't wait and want to sneak a peek.
2. You must stop when time is called unless you are not finished, in which case you may holler "I am not finished," and continue with the exam.

3. Use only a #2 pencil. If you didn't bring one, you may use a rollerball, gel, or ballpoint pen. You may *not* use the stylus from your PDA.

4. A cell phone on "silent ring mode" is permitted in the testing area. You may also bring your administrative assistant to help you with the exam. However, you may not bring any briefcases, purses, or backpacks into the testing area — although your assistant may carry them in for you.

DO NOT PROCEED.
WAIT FOR THE PROCTOR'S INSTRUCTIONS.

SECTION 1
Time: 30 minutes
Windows Professional Certification Exam for Executives:
Technical Proficiency

Directions:
This section of the exam tests your technical proficiency.

Complete all the questions in the section as quickly and accurately as you can. If you do not know the answer, move on. You have 30 minutes to complete this section.

BEGIN NOW.

Question 1:
What is the helpdesk's extension number at your company? _____

STOP HERE.
WAIT FOR THE PROCTOR'S INSTRUCTIONS.

Answer Key and Test Strategy *Although Section 1 accounts for less than a tenth of all questions, its weight on your overall score is a high 40 percent. This can make or break your attempt to get certified. To your benefit, the scoring is subjective and favors the certification candidate. For instance, in lieu of responding with the helpdesk's number, you may specify your organization's general reception number with a write-in addendum to "ask to be transferred to the helpdesk." But to receive full credit, you should know the extension or be able to read the speed-dial code from your cell phone's programmed directory. Scoring of this section is immediate. The proctor will initially review your answers. Those that represent "improbable" extensions (e.g., extensions containing letters not represented on a standard telephone like "Q" and "Z" or punctuation marks other than "*" and "#") will be scored as errors, and the candidate will be dismissed. All other answers will be presumed correct because, after all, you are an executive whose reputation is beyond reproach. Sometimes a proctor will ask the executive AA to verify the response and permit the AA to make necessary corrections. The key to scoring high in Section 1 is to not be hasty. Take your time, and work with your AA.*

SECTION 2
Time: 25 minutes
Windows Professional Certification Exam for Executives:
Leadership Skills

Directions:

This section of the exam tests the effectiveness of your leadership. Many times in your tenure, you will be called upon to achieve a particular objective. For instance, you may need to compel your entire organization to upgrade their workstations. How "efficiently" you accomplish this task (was it done on a weekend with little impact on productivity and was the target ROI achieved?) is less important than how "effectively" you accomplished this (i.e., did they carry out your orders?).

Complete the exercise and associated questions in the section, selecting the best answer from the choices as quickly and accurately as you can. If you do not know the answer, move on. You have 25 minutes to complete this section.

BEGIN NOW.

Exercise:

Discretely lean over toward your AA and ask him or her to bring you a coffee—lots of cream, lots of sugar.

Question 1:

Did your AA dutifully bring your coffee?

- (a) Yes
- (b) Yes, but he or she casually reminded me of the Microsoft Office certificate they earned from the local community college, implying "beverage server" was not part of *that* curriculum.
- (c) Yes, but in a Styrofoam cup, which I absolutely hate!
- (d) No, I got no coffee, but I *was* offered a Velamint with some purse lint on it.

Question 2:

If your AA *did* dutifully bring you coffee...

(a) Was it to your liking, as is proper?
(b) Did it have too much cream or too much sugar?
(c) Was it cold?
(d) Was it otherwise not to your preference, containing, for example, saccharin instead of aspartame or Coffeemate rather than cream?

STOP HERE.
YOU MAY NOT GO BACK TO PREVIOUS SECTIONS OR LOOK AHEAD. FINISH YOUR COFFEE (IF ONE WAS BROUGHT TO YOU) AND WAIT FOR THE PROCTOR'S INSTRUCTIONS.

Answer Key and Test Strategy This section's objective is to determine the level of unflinching loyalty you command over your subordinates. Because the success of a rollout (indeed, any project) depends highly on your authority to compel users to upgrade and your ability to wield that influence, many CEOs apportion a higher significance to this section than does the certification organization, which considers it only 15 percent of your overall exam score. Thus, you cannot afford to score poorly on this section.

The correct answer, then, for both questions is (a), even if it means you have to wince while sipping your coffee. To imply your subordinates are anything less than efficient loyalists can be tantamount to career suicide. You score this section yourself, though the proctor is instructed to look for erasures, which might suggest a level of impropriety (READ: inexcusable uncertainty) on your part.

SECTION 3
Time: 70 minutes
Windows Professional Certification Exam for Executives:
Expenditure Justification

Directions:

This final section of the exam tests your ability to justify a migration to the newest version of Windows. It calls on many of your executive skills to bring such a project to fruition.

This section contains three passages each followed by a series of questions. Read each passage carefully and complete the associated questions by selecting the best answer from the choices as quickly and accurately as you can. If you do not know the answer, move on. You have 70 minutes to complete this section.

BEGIN NOW.

Questions 1 through 4:

Read the passage, them complete the questions relating to it.

David Ladd is the VP of technology for Varnsön Industries, Inc., a manufacturing facility with approximately 300 workstations. Applications range from inventory control and shipping to product design. Ladd just received an e-mail from the director of purchasing. Apparently, all the new PCs ordered are being shipped with Windows 2000. To help manage resources, Ladd is considering migrating all users to Win2K. Such an upgrade involves not only additional licenses for existing workstations, but hardware upgrades, as well. Further, such an upgrade might disrupt the productivity of the entire organization. Still, Ladd believes the right thing to do is to centralize with a single operating system and chooses to move ahead. He has three days to prepare a presentation to the Varnsön board requesting not only additional funding, but also informing them of the possible risks of not meeting availability service levels.

Question 1:
Get your tin cup ready. The distilled version of your plea for additional funding is:

   (a) We budgeted for an upgrade next year, but it makes more sense to bite the bullet now.

(b) We were blind-sided by Microsoft's early release. We thought the "2K" in "Win2K" meant the year "2048."

(c) Living *La Vida Broka*: It's the cost of doing business in the changing world of IT.

Question 2:
One of the board members asks if an open source solution is not just cheaper, but is a viable alternative.

(a) "No," you say, babbling on about technological topics so far out of your comfort zone that the guy who comes in to trim the office plants shakes his head in disbelief.

(b) "No," you say, deferring explanation of the technical barriers to your support staff whose leader is, conveniently, out of town.

(c) "No," you say, waving-off the topic with "the support cost'll kill us."

(d) Admit that for most of the Minesweeper-playing workstation users, it probably would suffice, but more money could be saved on the support end—directing their attention to a real flashy pie chart on slide #14 of your PowerPoint presentation.

Question 3:
Dirk, a director representing the marketing leg of Varnsön, asks about Linux, claiming it's what everyone's talking about. You ...

(a) ... indicate simply that it's not in Varnsön's best interest, and leave it at that, recalling how you blew Question #2 by offering more information than necessary.

(b) ... sigh and page back a few slides, *again* pointing out the TCO of an OS with a bad UI and how little it benefits the organization.

(c) ... challenge Dirk: "Everyone's talking about it, Dirk? No one *here* is talking about it. You're the only one talking about it, Dirk. Say, I have an idea, why don't we let Dirk deliver this presentation?"

Question 4 (short essay):
In reality, the board will likely rubber-stamp anything you recommend because in the end, it is not the company's money, but your carcass that is on the line if the costs overrun or availability suffers. How do you CYA? (You may shoulder-read from the CIO in front of you and copy his answer if it is a good one.)

Question 5:
Read the following passage, then complete the question relating to it.

Windows 2000 introduces a host of new goodies including RIS, EFS, IpSec, and MMC. In terms of justifying the migration based on new features, the first thing you do is:

(a) Buy yourself the latest edition of an acronym dictionary.
(b) Focus your cost justification model on the features that don't sound like government agencies, for instance, improved security (file encryption and Kerberos support), accessibility tools for the impaired, and powerful new file-search facilities (but don't dwell on the latter—the 500-meg footprint of the OS pretty much implies files will be as hard to find as Nobel laureate Arno Penzias in the "For Dummies" aisle of Barnes & Noble.)

Questions 6 through 8:
Read the following passage then complete the questions relating to it.

Rod, your senior support technician, implores you to budget for additional support staff in your justification model, noting the almost-always higher-than-expected maintenance overhead (SP1, for example) as well as the other predictable support spikes his department sees with every IT change.

Question 6:
You...
(a) ... tell Rod the impact is only temporary, citing as evidence slide #14 of the aforementioned PowerPoint presentation.
(b) ... select (a), then decide to skip the last two questions in this section of the exam because you're getting hungry.

<u>Question 7:</u>
What was your answer for Question 6? _____

<u>Question 8:</u>
What was your answer for Question 7? _____

<u>Answer Key and Test Strategy:</u> This section of the exam carries the most weight toward your overall score, although it, like section one, is very subjective. The correctness of your answers is less important than how your own efforts play out—i.e., were you given the green light to go ahead with your own migration? Because there is no way to foretell, the certification organization understands how difficult it is to grade this section. So it is graded by exchanging your exam with the CIO next to you, who is likely to be just as interested in achieving a stellar score as you are.

STOP.
TURN IN ALL TEST MATERIALS TO YOUR PROCTOR.
YOU WILL RECEIVE YOUR CERTIFICATION AS SOON AS YOUR CHECK CLEARS.

ENJOY YOUR AFTERNOON.

Man on the street

"How important is it that the vendors you deal with are ISO-9000 certified?"

- "I have no idea ... my son's the computer wiz."
- "I'm just here to see if I can borrow some money from Bill Gates."
- "Do you know when the drawing is for the Jet-Ski?"
- "It's very, very important to us. What does ISO-9000 certified mean?"

—Asked at last month's IS Expo in Dallas

Why the AS/400 rocks

... by someone who knows absolutely nothing about it

I'm a science teacher. So why am I attempting to explain the AS/400's sustained success?

The magazine was looking for an "outside perspective" and no one is more out of it than my students; after all, the only technical discussions we typically have in class are the boys complaining the library's *Net Nanny* won't let them do "biology research" and the girls who are, "like whatEVER!"

But a little extra credit goes a long way towards mobilizing even the most clueless.

Here then, are extracts from my student's AS/400 research:

Zach G., 16 ("How am I driving? Dial 1-800-BITE-ME")

I was looking at this book about computers. One was the VIC-20, but there was, like, just a keyboard. I'm like, maybe someone tore out the rest of the page, but that was it. I guess the "VIC" part was short for "victim."

Next, I scoped a mainframe, but it reminded me too much of the cabinet my ol' man keeps his coats in.

Then I saw it: The AS/400. And it was good.

It was black, dark, coffeehouse Goth. And it had a CD-player. And I said, "This box rocks."

The end.

Alicia H., 15 ("16 in May")

OK, like, businesses use it. So it's important, right? But why do businesses use it?

They use it because it's what all the "suits" read about on airplanes.

The question, Mr. Stewart, is not *why* the AS/400 is so popular, but "How long will it *stay* popular?"

I mean, like, we're the next generation of execs, right? If we had to decide now what would be on tomorrow's corporate desktops—Intel workstations or Sony PlayStations—I'll tell you we wouldn't have that little Microsoft paper clip telling us what to do.

So, for the AS/400 to "sustain" its "market share," those guys need to look at *our* bio info and advertise in, like, *Vibe* and *Seventeen*. Maybe have *e.r.*'s Doug Ross treat a kid who had a mainframe fall on him, and he could say something like, "Kid, you should have had an AS/400 fall on you. You would be better off, and ... by the way, don't you think Alicia H. is cute?"

That would be cool to a lot of us, and we would buy AS/400's because George Clooney told us to.

Matt F., 14 [he claims, we suspect, to avoid being tried as an adult]

OK, IBM has these three platforms, right? OS/2, OS/390, and OS/400. Well, duh, isn't it obvious? The biggest number is the best. I mean, if I get a 62 percent on a test, I'm a lot smarter than someone who just got a 60 percent.

Thank you.

Erin P., 16 ("Drug-Free, That's Me!")

I did some web searches, and apparently, I'm the only one so far with hard facts:

Web hits for the 400: 1,665,220; NT: 1,417,720; MVS: 58,310.

Now let's talk about languages. RPG: 94,510; COBOL: 43,930.

Those're facts, Mr. Stewart, not conjecture, speculation, assumption, extrapolation, or theorization [Erin has recently discovered the thesaurus feature of Word].

The AS/400 rocks because it's the buzz. It's what everyone's talking about!

That's all I have to say, thanks for listening, and I hope everyone can make my party on Saturday.

Matt F., 14

I would like to append my earlier presentation ...

Y'know how speakers have a woofer, tweeter, and a midrange? Well, you can do without the first two, but without a kickin' midrange, you're listening to high-pitched whining and aneurysmic thumping.

Do you see the connection? In a data center, you have big iron and little PCs. But in the middle, you have what you can't do without! The work horse.

That's why they call the AS/400 a "midrange!"

I yield the remaining time to my distinguished colleague from American History 201.

John L., 16 ("Go Green Bay!")

The popularity of the 400 is in its limitations, not its abilities. Its bold un-pretension is the appeal.

Think about it. Its chief competition is NT, which you need to reboot, like, six times a day. Besides that, if you were a manager, and I'm asking my fellow students to really stretch your imagination for a minute and pretend you are a mature adult, would you want your organization relying on a machine that runs *Redneck Rampage* and *The Babysitters Club Activity Center*?

No chat rooms. No AOL buddy lists. Just work. The 400's strictly business.

OK, you can suspend your imaginations now. I'm through.

Matt F., 14

Dude, I saw myself in a necktie there for a minute. I'm gonna kick your butt after class for making me go through that.

Jeremy L., 15 ("I don't care if you don't like my hair, *I* don't have to look at it!")

The 400 rocks because of its programming simplicity. A machine's only as good as the software that runs on it. And on no platform is it easier to write applications then on the 400.

To wit: in most environments, you have to create requirements, design the application, write the code, inspect, compile, test, and debug the program.

But on the on the 400, you do none of that. There is this one "awesome" command, CRTRPGPGM.

That's way cool.

So what have we concluded class? The AS/400 is a successful business machine because it's a cool-looking box that doesn't run *You Don't Know Jack*? And that IBM better start marketing it to teen-agers or the next generation of CIOs will be running mission critical application on a Nintendo platform?

Class?

Anyone?

Matt F., 14

Is any of this gonna be on the test?

... And I would like to thank my intelligent software agent

This year's Oscars left few surprises. Billy Crystal did his typical played-out shtick, Elke Sommer got snubbed yet another year for the Thalberg award, and Red Buttons was in the bathroom when he was supposed to be presenting. (In what might have been the highlight of the night, Buttons later walked on the Shrine Auditorium stage—interrupting and upstaging Warren Beatty—blamed his condition on the pre-award party *hors d'oeuvres*, clutched his stomach with one hand and the seat of his pants with the other, and ran back offstage to a roar of laughter.)

What *was* a surprise, at least for the pocket protector crowd, were the great numbers of technical kudos relegated to the less glamorous ceremony the night before. This year, several IT-related awards were added, as well, and as was typical, they didn't garner nearly the attention they deserved. So, in the interest of paying the appropriate respect to those in our industry, we present those award winners.

Best RPG Code in a Supporting Role

The Best RPG Code in a Supporting Role award went to the subroutine, "CALC_IT," which was used in the production accounting program for the Dustin Hoffman sequel *Outbreak II: The Good Times Virus*. Bill Radimacky, a Warner Brothers senior programmer analyst, accepted the award thanking the academy, his parents, and the guy who keeps the Mountain Dew machine stocked.

Best Algorithm in a Major Motion Picture

This one was anyone's guess. The critics liked the dark element of *Ma and Pa Kettle Log Off* while an Internet poll had the fans giving the nod to *Honey I Shrunk Your Butt With My New Scanner and Photo Editing Software*. But in the end, this award was all about computer-generated special effects, and that was clear when the ballots were tallied. James Cameron's *Witness II* took home the gold. Susan Hellmold accepted the award for developing the CAD program used to design the structure for the $150-million barn-raising scene.

Best Non-Commercial Exploitation of a Classic Film

It was tight running for all of these corporate instructional videos, each vying to keep employee attention by using a hackneyed twist on a classic film. But it was presenter Wink Martindale, venerable host of the 1980s TV classic "Tic Tac Dough," who had their attention when he opened the envelope and hollered, "A brand new car." After apologizing, "I just couldn't resist," he read off the winner in the category, *The Incredible Shrinking Benefits Package*, a video explaining how all employees and employers must both share the burden of rising health care costs. Julie Linderman accepted the award on behalf of the benefits department of Montgomery Ward acknowledging their tough competition this year: from Microsoft, *National Lampoon's You Can't Take Your Vacation Because Our Project's Behind Schedule*, and *Gentlemen Prefer Blondes*, a sexual harassment instructional indie film commissioned by the EEOC's HR department.

Best Commercial Exploitation of a Classic Film

Though they took out full-page ads in the trades for their *Herbie Gets OnStar*, General Motors knew it was the underdog, and there was little surprise when IBM won for their film-short *AS/401 Dalmatians*, which spokesperson Mary Tiernehey claimed "would do for the AS/400 what Charlie Chaplin did for the PC Jr," a speech that got the evening's only standing ovation ... from a row of Windows marketeers.

Best Help Desk Support

There were no nominees in this category.

Best Adaptation of a Made-for-TV or Direct-to-Video movie into a Webcast

Going in with two paws up from PC Week's *Spence the Katt* and a showing at Sundance (albeit covert), Martial Law's Sammo Hung-produced *Mr. Moto and the Denial of Service Attack* was expected to be the shoe-in of the night. But when the envelope was opened, the statuette went to the writers of *Barbarians at the Gates'*, a humorous tale of Bill and Melinda Gates being mistaken for squatters by their own security staff while living in a double-wide trailer on the construction site of their $50 million Lake Washington estate. Ahh, Oscar can be unpredictable when he wants to be, and no one knows that better than fellow nominees Mary-Kate and Ashley Olsen, whose *Mary-Kate & Ashley's Silicon Valley Adventure* was panned by the academy this year. "We're just happy being nominated," one of them said. "Yeah, it's a privilege being in such great company," the other said before both ran off crying to their mother.

Award hoopla aside, the highlight of the evening was the presentation of the prestigious "Bob Fazzarri Lifetime Achievement Award." This year's recipient was Hollywood IT consultant Paul Flerik who managed to leverage the literal meaning of his "Year-2K" on-call support for the *Scream, Friday the 13th*, and *Halloween* franchises. Flerik gets a monthly check through the year 2048 regardless of actual production.

The Lifetime Achievement Award was named for the legendary Hollywood goldbrick Bob Fazzarri who worked the same three story lines into a writing career spanning more than thirty years and some forty-five *Laurel and Hardy* and *Abbott and Costello* feature films. Asked one day back in the 50s as to the secret of his prolificacy, he replied, "Cut and Paste, baby ... cut and paste!"

The top six Google search terms...

... as reported by Mrs. Farkel's second-grade class

1. Michael Jordan
2. Power Rangers
3. Pog
4. Boogers
5. Dinosaurs
6. Dinosaur Boogers

Old characters never die ...
they just consult

The success of *The Brady Bunch Movie, Charlie's Angels*, and *Star Trek XVII Where No Man Has Gone Before: Kirk Gets a Colonoscopy* proves we just can't get enough of good characters.

That Hollywood's creative juices flow like molasses is further demonstrated by a slough of new streamed webcasts designed to exploit not only the success of television and movie icons, but their "Gen-Hex" audience, as well.

Here are samples of some of the new shows we'll be watching in little one and a half inch windows on our desktops.

The Professor and Mary Ann, LLP

In this colossal waste of bandwidth the two castaways start an island consulting business. Sample dialog:

Mary Ann: Professor, how will we ever manage to wire Mr. Howell's PC to the Skipper's server?

Professor: I've fashioned an acoustic coupler out of some coconut shells. The Howells should be online in no time.

Mary Ann: That's great, but don't stand so close to me when we talk, it makes me feel uncomfortable.

Professor: No problem. By the way, I've moved the sexual harassment complaint forms to the bottom drawer of my desk.

Columbo, Kojak, and Fish, Inc.

Hollywood wisely cast these characters as a *Space Cowboys*-type tiger team. Whether or not viewers will enjoy their octogenarian escapades remains to be seen. Sample banter:

Columbo: OK, let me think here for a moment. You say you have a problem booting your PC, sir. But what I don't understand ... errr, you don't mind if I smoke ... You say the first time it failed to boot, you were in the lunchroom. Is that right, sir?

Fish: I said I was in the bathroom, not the lunchroom.

Columbo: I'm asking the client.

Fish: Oh.

Columbo: Sir, did it ever occur to you that this diskette in the A: drive might be what's prohibiting you from booting? I think you'll find that if you ... if you'll just indulge me for a moment ... sir ...

Columbo ejects the diskette.

Columbo: ... pop this disk out and reboot! *Voila*!

Kojak takes the Tootsie-Pop out of his mouth.

Kojak: Cock-a-doodle-do, sweetheart!

Scooby Doo and Associates

Many of today's propeller heads weren't even born when this bunch first hit the celluloid, but the popularity of the mystery-solving group has not waned since. With a well-defined demographic audience, this one's a definite contender. Sample mystery:

Fred and Shaggy are talking.

Fred: So I said, "If the Mystery Machine's a rockin', don't come a-knockin'."

The rest enter.

Velma: OK, gang, Mr. Chandler says his computer is doing things by itself. He thinks it's possessed.

Shaggy: Possessed?

Scooby: Rikes!

Shaggy: You can say that again, Scoob!

Scooby: Rikes!

Fred: Relax you two. When a computer does things by itself, it's not a ghost, it's just a virus.

Shaggy: Like, that's easy for you to say.

Shaggy and Scooby approach the PC and apprehensively double-click on an icon. A desktop window maximizes and a fiendish character's head pops out of the window coming face to face with them. They freeze in terror.

Shaggy: *(shaking)* It's just a virus. It's just a virus.

Scooby: Rust a rirus. Rust a rirus.

The fiend unleashes a massive sneeze on Shaggy.

Shaggy: Like, zoinks, Scoob! Let's make like a runny nose and blow!

As the two bolt from the cubicle, the program segues to a McAfee commercial.

The Patch Adams, Quincy, and Hathaway Group

What do you get when three of the most regarded medical professionals work to save a production system? Must see TV. Let's see:

Adams: What do we have here, Nurse Hathaway?

Hathaway: Two-year old AS/400 530-series, V4.R3, exhibits signs of decreased system performance. I'm waiting to hear back from the leasing company to see what their warranty will cover.

Adams: Never mind that, get me a pair of metric slip-joint pliers, a #2 Phillips head screwdriver, and some 30-weight ball-bearings. Dr. Quincy, your thoughts?

Quincy: Don't ask me. I only work on the dead ones.

Sound effect: Flatline tone.

Hathaway: Oh, God, it's hemorrhaging data. I think it's a runaway DASD.

Adams: Looks like your services might come in handy here after all, Quincy. I'll be right back. I need to get my clown nose.

Hathaway: What do we do, Dr. Quincy?

Quincy walks over to the electrical outlet and kicks out the power cord. Sound effect: DASD winding down.

Quincy: Call it.

Hathaway: Eleven-o-five.

Quincy: I think we could both use a drink.

Hathaway nods. The camera freezes as Quincy takes her hand, then pans to the incapacitated AS/400. The end credits roll.

Corleone, Kirkland, Montana, Brigante and Wortzik Consulting

Finally, take an amalgam of Al Pacino characters and make them consultants for a mobile help desk, and what do you get? Unfortunately, if the promos are any indication, you get a chunk of wasted disk cache. Sample excerpt:

Wortzik: ... no, I can't stoop down and look at the router 'cause of my bad back. Sciatica! Sciatica!

Corleone: We are all reasonable men, we can come together and find a solution to this Ethernet problem.

Montana: I say we blow that !#*@%ing Ethernet card back to !#*@%ing Silicon Valley where it !#*@%ing came from.

Kirkland: Look at this documentation. This page is out of order; that page is out of order. This whole !#*@%ing manual is out of order!

Brigante: ¡Tranquila! ¡Tranquila! The PCMCIA card just needs to be reseated.

Montana: ¡Oye! The card is stuck inna slot? Daz you problem? (*Montana whips out his multi-purpose pocket-tool*) Say hello to my *leetle* friend!

They all laugh as the toll-free support number scrolls across the bottom of the screen.

Believe it or not...

Someone working in the claims processing division of a large insurance company in Illinois actually added paper to the department's laser printer before the "out-of-paper" alert sounded.

Big brother is watching

One

It was a weekday afternoon like any other when Winston Smith pushed aside a spent frozen meal and drew a small disk from his shirt pocket. He typically spent his sixty-minute lunch sabbatical in his cube reading or playing a game of solitaire to purge his mind of the morning stress and to prepare himself for more of the same in the afternoon.

Though his breaks were often interrupted by phone calls or urgent e-mails, he was pleased to serve the company which was paying for his house, financing his son's viola lessons, and had paid for his daughter's braces. Even if it was at the expense of his personal time. On this particular day, Winston had only a mere ten minutes to himself. But ten minutes was all he needed to finish the eText of George Orwell's *1984* that he had been reading for the past month—a book he last read some twenty years ago in high school. Well, actually, he would confess, a book whose *CliffsNotes* he last read some twenty years ago in high school; and if pressed, admitted he probably just skimmed those.

One o'clock was approaching, and Winston was beginning to focus on his afternoon task list when an urgent e-mail arrived. It was from what Winston would later call the *Ministry of Compliance*, but for now was just known as human resources. It was another of what seemed like an increasing number of company policy changes. This week, the memo read, Winston's company, like many other Fortune

1000 companies, was deploying employee-monitoring software to log every character typed, every application executed, every radio-button selected. All in the name of employee productivity. The e-mail closed thanking the staff for their continued loyalty and hard work.

Winston felt betrayed. At first, it was just the memo's "newspeak" of calling his PC a "workstation," removing any indication that it was his *personal* computer. But then a revelation came: it was not the Orwellian government he needed to fear, but private industry. The government wasn't tracking every item he charged or every grocery item he bought with his *super-saver club card*. The government wasn't maintaining and renting his personal data, bank balances, and medical history. And the government, certainly, wasn't logging his every keystroke.

"Oh my God," Winston muttered, "I am working for Ingsoc, Inc."

Two

Winston was angry. Angry at the very organization where for two decades there existed a bond—a social contract—of mutual trust and respect. He became disillusioned and sought the camaraderie of the brotherhood—those who often filled their briefcases with lunchroom coffee packets and auctioned-off pilfered office supplies on eBay.

Emmanuel Goldstein worked in the shipping department and was well-regarded as a disgruntled employee. Or was that merely a rumor? Since the great reorg of 1997 you could never gauge the loyalty of a coworker. Some believed Goldstein actually worked for the *Ministry of Ordinance* (corporate security) and would rat-out those who came to him for tips on using the company postage meter to mail their holiday cards or other infractions against the larger holding company.

But he had to be sure.

One afternoon, Winston happened upon Goldstein brushing his teeth in the restroom. He hesitated, then blurted, "This place bites."

What was he thinking? If Goldstein was, indeed, a stooge for the holding company, Winston had committed the equivalent of career suicide. He backed down, "I mean ..."

"The new policy?" Goldstein said. "I'm surprised they don't have Webcams in the stalls."

They shared a laugh, and Winston breathed a sigh of relief. "So there are disgruntled employees here. It's true?"

"Yes, we don't appreciate the specter of the holding company looking over our shoulders. It's counterproductive." Goldstein went on: "Isn't it rather asinine to tell a developer who's working 14-hour days that at 8:00 P.M. he cannot make a personal call to tell his wife he has to stay even later?"

The tenet of the brotherhood, Goldstein explained, was to let an employee's performance, not Machiavellian surveillance, speak for itself. But that would be difficult under the cloud of suspicion that monitoring presented. If Winston was to truly buy-in to the brotherhood, Goldstein said, he should continue his exemplary performance, but when the urge to *decompress* manifested itself, Winston needed to do so without the aid of the organization's workstation.

"When you want to read," Goldstein began, "you read lowtech. No eText. No CNN.com. For you, it's hardcovers and *USA Today*. They'll be watching for idle keyboard time. So you'll need to get one of those old drinking bird toys that bob their beaks up and down. Position it to bop the page down key of the longest corporate policy document you can load in Word, then go on about reading. Anyone auditing your workstation will be impressed at your conscientiousness.

"Feel like a game of solitaire? Again, low-tech is the future. A deck of cards still works. Pack one in your briefcase ... next to the bird. And buy yourself a yo-yo and learn how to use it.

"E-commerce? It'll die on the vine. Sure, the web site may be secure, but if your keystrokes are monitored, any Kojak-wannnabe in the *Ministry of Ordinance* will have access to your information. So no more ordering online, or even on the phone. It's off to the store like the old days. You'll need to carve an hour out of the work day to do that ... a hard drive defrag ought to keep their monitoring software busy."

Goldstein went on for what seemed like an hour, indoctrinating Winston. Though Winston needed little convincing, he left with an even stronger conviction that employee monitoring would set technology back twenty-five years and eradicate the concept of company loyalty. Morale and productivity would eventually go by the wayside as well.

He hated his job and the holding company for what it had driven him to become. He knew what he had to do next.

Three

[This section has been deleted by the *Ministry of Pettiness* as it has been determined that it was conceived, though during the author's permitted lunch break, on company premises using company-provided ventilation and is thus the intellectual property of Ingsoc, Inc. The author has been counseled on this matter.]

Four

Winston arrived at Ingsoc, Inc. precisely at 7:00 A.M.

He opened his briefcase and removed several manila folders on which he had worked the night before. He spread them out and opened his cluttered Filofax to plan his day.

He rolled his chair back a bit to survey the mounds of work that would surely keep him busy into the late evening and leaned back.

As he began opening the accumulated e-mails, Winston said under his breath, "I love my job."

What Google tells us about ourselves ...

John Hume & David Trimble, 1998 Nobel Prize in Peace: 606 hits.
Southpark's Mr. Hankey: 811.

"Get your modem running ..."

When Technodyne CIO Merl Haberman was invited to present before an international technical steering committee on the topic of remote access problems he didn't really think there was much to report because from his perspective things were fine in his organization.

But when he learned his department had used-up most of its travel budget three months before it would be refreshed, he needed to get from Chicago to L.A. "on the cheap."

The experience proved to be an eye-opening one as Merl experienced first-hand the role remote access plays in day-to-day business operations and how difficult it is to stay connected on the road.

This is his journal.

Chicago bus station, Saturday morning

I'm off to a bad start when told there are no seats available directly to L.A. But out of this adversity comes opportunity to exercise the technology. I spy an available telephone jack, quickly connect to the bus line's webpage, and plot myself a route through Minneapolis securing the necessary reservations with my credit card.

At our first rest stop, I locate a phone jack to check my office email. I have nine. I send myself an email that is immediately acknowledged by my autoresponder indicating I am out of the office. I get another "RE: RE:" then another "RE: RE: RE:" I get them *ad infinitum*, or at least *"ad until I am disconnected."* Apparently my autoresponder is carrying out a conversation with itself.

I phone the help desk, and after 20 minutes on hold, I am given the service number 39712 and a promise of a callback.

Back in line to check-in, the clerk is coercing me to sign-up for their frequent rider program. I need more plastic in my wallet like I need another free AOL disk, but the lure of a free upgrade to sit in the seat up front next to the driver after only 5000 miles is too compelling.

On the bus, I perform a "handshake loop" test to see if my technological ducks are all in a row. From my PCS cellular phone, I call my office phone where there is no answer; the call then rolls to my cell phone which is, of course, busy; finally it rolls to the pager in my pocket. The passenger in the seat next to me misinterprets my giggle of satisfaction from the pager's vibration and moves to another seat.

Mauston, Wisconsin, same day

Another setback. While waiting in line to buy one of those souvenir foam cheese-head hats, the bus leaves without me.

I quickly phone my boss who's away from his desk but was kind enough to still have his phone forwarded to mine from when he was on vacation three weeks ago. A moment later, my pager goes off.

I reluctantly accept a ride from a van of college students with a mutual need. I need to go west. They need a designated driver.

Outside Rapid City, South Dakota

When Joshua spills a beer on Dylan because of some undocumented potholes I encounter near Mt. Rushmore, a dispute erupts over the currency of my CD-ROM road atlas, and I am unceremoniously thrown out of the van.

It is 3:05 A.M. and against my better judgment, I accept a ride from a small gang of Sturgis bikers *en route* to Provo to, as Viper says, "raise some hell" at a Novell User's Conference regarding a user interface enhancement request they submitted five month ago. I think they're just making it up, but they have pool cues and look like they're not afraid to use them, so I just let it go.

Salt Lake City

I bid Viper, Switchblade, Lockdown, and their women farewell as they leave me and my rattled viscera at a car rental agency.

I try to connect to my LAN, but this time I am getting a busy signal. I suspect a shortage of ports on our remote server and phone the help desk for confirmation. After twenty minutes of elevator music and a taped update on yesterday's system crippling email loop, I speak to a human who gives me Service Number 40312 and a callback promise.

The middle of nowhere

"Hell of a place to run out of gas," I mumble while dialing the rental agency's 24-hour help line only to be told *I* must be doing something wrong because *their* car starts just fine and maybe I should read the owner's manual before I call them the next time. To say I told them "thank you" is only half true.

I try the motor club and barely give them the number of my PCS phone when its lighted display flickers, then dies.

I walk perhaps six miles along the highway before the 5.2 pound notebook starts to become burdensome, though I do enjoy listening to my CDs along the way on it.

I find a pay-phone whose handset is lying in the sand ten feet away. I can't be sure, but it look like it was severed with a shotgun blast. I manage to work what's left of the phone away from its mounting and connect my modem line to an exposed jack. I construct an email to the motor club designating my PCS phone as the return address because of the aforementioned auto-responder fiasco. No sooner do I press the send button than the notebook shuts down, its batteries, too, have breathed their last.

I walk for another two miles looking to shed unnecessary ballast. I am seconds away from jettisoning the cheese hat when I hear the sound of an approaching convoy. One of them screeches to a halt.

I share my frustration with battery capacity and my immediate need to find a pay phone for our weekly budget review. "B.J." is sympathetic to my predicament and soon, with the help of a network of his good buddies, I'm on the C.B. with Grice in our Atlanta office and Jurczak in Dallas where I'm asked to approve an upgrade for one of our routers. I approve saying, "That's a big 10-4, good buddy."

Flagstaff, Arizona

At a truck stop in Flagstaff, I successfully connect to the LAN, but one of the application updates that's automatically distributed over the network hoses my mail app. I try to call the help desk again. I'm on hold for forty minutes then get cut off.

Mother always warned me about people who have license plate frames made from chain, but this fellow who offered me a ride in the back of his pick-up truck seemed OK.

While hanging on for dear life, my phone rings with an email from the auto club confirming someone is on the way. A minute later, I get another email from the motor club inviting me to upgrade to their "gold" membership. Five seconds later, I get another offering me their Visa card. I don't believe it, I'm getting spammed on my PCS phone!

Somewhere in Arizona

I'm standing on a corner in Winslow, Arizona, and I'm in no mood to sing the rest of the song. I was just thrown from the bed of the pickup truck while the driver executed what I would call an evasive maneuver. Fortunately, my notebook is intact. My ribs broke its fall.

A family in a station wagon on the way to Disneyland picks me up, but I don't know what's worse, the children bickering and crying or the father's empty threat to "pull over the car and give them something to cry about."

Stopped at a train crossing near Albuquerque, I spot the solution for my agony: an open boxcar.

"It's not exactly first class," Georgia Pete acknowledges, "but for two bits I can throw some hay in the corner and call it business class."

I have never been in a boxcar before. I suppose what impresses me most is the home office he's fashioned from old appliance boxes. "I don't do much in there," he says, "I just maintain it for the tax deduction."

Las Vegas

While my phone battery is charging in the buffet, I try my luck in the casino. Three hours later, after a binge at the craps table, I am wiped-out.

I find a dime on the carpet of the Flamingo and on the second pull, hit the progressive slot for $65 in nickels. Enough to buy a bus ticket to San Bernardino.

I grab my recharged phone that had since accumulated seven emails: four touting MLM opportunities, two hawking diet plans, and one that had the nerve to tell me about bargain air fares from Chicago to L.A. "as cheap as riding the rails." I wonder is there's a camera somewhere.

After an hour on the bus overhearing a conversation between Wayne behind me and Myrna across the aisle from him who apparently worked as a "professional fantasy dancer" named Candy Corn, I have a fantasy of my own. It goes like this: I open my notebook and boot it up; a hand then appears holding a pistol and puts me out of my misery.

I tell myself they're all probably harmless, but to be on the safe side, I spend the rest of the ride with my hand on my wallet hoping I don't fall asleep. To keep myself awake, I call the help desk to ask why they don't ever get back to me. My query is assigned Service Number 39712. Before I can say, "Hey, I already have that number," they hang-up.

San Bernardino, Wednesday morning

A kind fellow here offers me a ride to LA. Apparently, he needs another "body" so he can ride in the car pool lane. I am uneasy with the way he says "body," but I am in a pickle and take him up on his offer.

I try my boss again, but he's not in and *still* hasn't changed his forwarding. Now I need to explain the pager vibration to Mitch who apparently installs cable systems in homes only I get the impression the cable companies don't know he does.

We discuss technology and have an interesting conversation until we break on the benefits GPS applications. I am about to argue until I notice the electronic monitoring device welded around his ankle. You don't want argue with the president of the Attica debating team, or at least that's what his tattoo says.

I ask him where he learned so much about technology. He laughed and said if he told me he would have to kill me. I chuckled nervously. I got the impression he was going to kill me anyway and all the police would have to go on were the queued emails on my phone advertising topless Eastern European supermodels.

A moment later, we came face-to-face with one of those infamous LA traffic jams.

East Los Angeles, next day

We move up two car lengths.

Los Angeles, Friday next day

I'm in town for about five minutes when my laptop is actually stolen ... *right off my laptop.* I dial 911, but while I'm on hold, an operator interrupts informing me I am calling from a phone which "has apparently been cloned and will be prevented by fraud detection software from originating any more calls."

But I think it'll all be worth it. I have accumulated three pages of notes outlining the downsides to staying connected on the road. As I approach the meeting room, I primp my 6-day old appearance reviewing my recommendations: more remote LAN connection ports, back-up batteries, a good support staff ...

Notes in hand, I enter the conference room apologizing for my disheveled appearance. But the room is empty. There is just a small camera and a television monitor set-up. I don't believe it; I traveled two-thousand miles to attend a teleconference!

But there is little time to reflect on this paradox. I have to be back in my office tomorrow afternoon for a conference call.

The I.T. advisor ...

... dispensing counsel on technology, online romance, and other vital topics since February of last year.

Dear Advisor,

I have been carrying-on an email relationship with a woman on the net, Debbie295, for two months, and I would like to take it to the next level: a Webcam meeting. Unfortunately, I have a dial-up connection, and my NetMeeting video is choppy. My feelings of bandwidth inadequacy leave me apprehensive. Should I instead build an animated GIF and email that?

—Dale from Ft. Lauderdale

Dale:

A French muse once wrote, *"Frère Jacques, Frère Jacques, Dormez vous? Dormez vous?"* which loosely translated means, "Jack, do you know if the girls' dorms are really any different than ours except for the brassieres on the floor?"

Don't for a moment think that lil' Debbie295 isn't having the same reservations. Whether she has broadband access or a dial-up connection, she's worried you'll learn she's not all she makes herself out to be. The advisor himself once had quite the heated relation with one alleged Susan1141 who claimed to be a 23-year-old dead-ringer for Jennifer Anniston. But after a photo exchange, it was clear that she meant she looked like an exhumed Jennifer Anniston, dead for 23 years.

Think about this: somewhere out there is a software nerd trying to impress an online hottie by bragging that he wrote the microcode that drives the Big Mouth Billy Bass animatronics. Frightening, huh?

If your biggest shortcoming is your net connection, count yourself lucky.

Dear Advisor,

Last week I received an email with the subject "Good Times Virus." I was always a big fan of the show and I wanted to find out if either of my two favorite characters, Willona or Florida, took ill. Well, the next thing you know, my desktop is corrupted, my hard drive is erased, and I have gingivitis. What's up?

—Moe from Palermo

Moe:

The German songsmith, Nena, sang, *"Hast du etwas zeit fuer mich, ein emial, cc: von 99 luftballons"* which using all the German the advisor picked up from reruns of "Hogan's Heroes" means, when you exchange email with someone, you are exchanging email with everyone *that* person has emailed as far back as 99 cc's.

But here's the good news. You can't get a virus just by opening an email. You have to actually open an attachment. Though one insidious email making the rounds called "The Lazy Guy's Virus," includes this viral text in the body of the email:

"This virus works on the honor system;

Please forward this message to everyone you know ...

Then, if you would, please delete all the files on your hard drive ...

Finally, please forward this email to everyone in your address book.

Thank you for your cooperation."

Dear Advisor,

I am a second lieutenant in the U.S. Army assigned to the Pentagon's data processing department. Here's my dilemma. Our department recently adopted a "casual Friday" uniform dress policy, but I just have so little to coordinate. Can you help a government employee with a small uniform allowance look like a runway model?

—Mark (originally from) Bismarck

Mark:

Legend has it when a Roman soldier asked whether it was better to buy an unneeded tunic to be prepared for a time in the field when such a garment would come in handy, or if it would be more prudent to stock-up on rations for similar preparedness, the old philosopher, Vinny Viddivicci, told him, *"Carpe per diem,"* or "the fish swim each day." In other words, you can always get a meal, but for that snappy set of threads in the window, the sale ends Wednesday.

Casual Friday in the military is an emerging trend. Thus, anything goes—white undershirt or olive-drab undershirt; polyester or 60/40 poly/cotton blend—it all depends how wacky you feel.

There is really just one steadfast rule: don't wear camouflage Arctic whites after Labor Day.

Dear Advisor,

Last Christmas, our office party got a little out of hand and, to make a long story short, I landed up on the office copier with a contractor. My problem is that my employer is claiming rights to my little bundle of joy due in September. Where do I stand?

—Sue from Sioux Falls

Sue,

First off all, be thankful the copier wasn't one of those stapling models. But seriously, junior might, in fact, legally belong to your employer if you signed a standard employment agreement assigning all "ideas, creations, and inventions designed, created, or conceived on company time, premises, or using company-provided hardware." The key is whether you are classified as hourly or exempt. If you're hourly, and the *collation* took place outside of your normal working hours, the creation is yours. If, however, you're salaried, you have no defined work hours, and it can be argued the output of on-premise activities are the property of your employer. That your partner is a consultant further complicates the matter. You should consult a lawyer specializing in the labor laws of your state.

Don't quote me

"Nobody's on AOL anymore, the line's always busy."

—*Yogiberra@aol.com*

Fonts throughout history

In a 3270- or 5250-device world where typographers, on their most generous day, might call the green screens "purposefully eloquent," it is hard for programmers to grasp the prominence fonts have had throughout history. But as sure John Hancock hogged the Declaration of Independence with his 78-point New Berolina MT signature, fonts have left their mark on our civilization.

"Let there be Arial Light!"

The origin of fonts, as we know them, has been the topic of heated debate. For most of recorded history, man presumed they had simply always existed. But in the late 19th century, science proposed its own explanation and in 1925, that diametrically-opposed theory of font origin clashed in what was coined the "Scopes F-Key Trial."

Arguing for typesetter John Scopes in a civil trial, famed litigator Clarence Darrow claimed uppercase characters evolved from lowercase characters. William Jennings Bryan held firm to the common notion that capital letters were "like the F-keys on a PC, always there!"

But the battle would not be limited to words. At one point in the trial, Bryan threw a rolled sock in Darrow's direction hollering, "There, what do you think of that?" Darrow took a moment to confer with his client then responded by lobbing a compressed handkerchief on Bryan's legal pad.

Eventually, the most damning testimony on the origin of up-percase characters would come from one of Bryan's own witnesses, e. e. cummings, who shocked the packed courtroom by drunkenly recanting an earlier statement and instead citing a statistic that cockroaches outnumbering humans "does not necessarily make them a superior species."

Judge Raulston declared a mistrial "on account of no one knows what the hell cummings just said," leaving the matter forever unre-solved.

"Write like an Egyptian (oh, way oh)"

The true origin of type notwithstanding, the enigma surround-ing Egyptian text has mesmerized man for millenniums.

Though many had tried to understand the mysterious car-touches, it was Napoleon's troops in 1799 who discovered a key to deciphering the wisdom of the ages locked in the cryptic glyphs. In a basalt tablet found in the town of Rosetta was a message written in several languages, one of them the elusive ancient hieroglyphic font.

Napoleon engaged a young mathematician named Jean-François Champollion to crack the code using secret supercomputers housed in the basement of the Bastille.

For two years, Champollion toiled ... then came a breakthrough. The text, Champollion learned, was not encoded at all. It was simply an 18-point Zapf Dingbat. When the enterprising young man did a *Select All* and changed the font to Bookman Old Style the epoch-old words rung again:

> **High Priest Nebwenenef:** "How many slaves does it take to build a pyramid?"
>
> **High Priest Imhotep:** "I dunno. How many?"
>
> **High Priest Nebwenenef:** "Two hundred thousand. Ten to cut the stone and 199,990 to drag it up to Giza."
>
> **High Priest Imhotep:** "Not funny. Now finish tell-ing me how that alabaster-futures multi-level marketing scheme of yours is going to make us all rich."

"Brother Anthony has to go!"

For nearly three thousand years, fonts remained relatively unremarkable. Friars and professional scriveners made extensive use of Old English MT, Symbol, and Script MT Bold. But in 1440 AD, two significant trends rocked the *status quo*.

Owing to an arthritis epidemic, monks began right-sizing-out the older robed brethren because no one could read their handwriting; young freelance writers filled-in. About the same time, former carny weight-guesser Johannes Gutenberg introduced a new Courier font to the public that he called, oddly enough, Courier New, which permitted the mass publication of materials.

For the first time, illiterate cabbage-pickers could now join the educated elite in producing and enjoying some of the great literary masters for the masses. Popular titles of the time included *Beowatch*, *Vasco Da Gama's Collection of Bawdy Jokes*, and *Bloodletting for Dummies*.

... and then there were those who couldn't tell their slash from their elbow

Back in the days of old California, graffiti was a perplexing thing. Fonts of the time did not make a distinction between some characters. For instance, the capital letter "O" and the number "0" were strikingly similar.

Such was the bane of Capistrano. Someone, apparently, was leaving "number two" on many government buildings.

For months, the poor pueblo peons were confused. Was this some sort of gang symbol or a celebration of incontinence?

It was, of course, just the mark of Don Diego's alter ego, Zorro. Diego eventually returned to his native Spain—disillusioned with the ignorance of the people he was trying to help—but not before leaving just one last mark, this time introducing a small slash to distinguish it from the number two:

No one ever learned the identity of the hombre who left the "mark of the number two with a small slash in it," but one guard reported seeing a man flee who "looked like that guy from *Lost in Space*."

Times Modern

Today, there appears to be no sign of diminishing fascination with fonts. If anything, the advent of PCs has caused us to embrace type even more so, integrating it into our pop culture. Television is replete with font tributes. We have *Adobe Gillis*, *The Life and Times Roman of Grizzly Adams*, and the popular sci-fi show *Battlestar Helvetica*. And if popular music is any barometer, we are clearly a society that is *hooked on fontics*. From the malaise-induced standard of desktop publishers *You Can't Always Get the Right Font* and the reggae classic *I Shot the Serif* to that ode to diacriticals *Waltzing Matilde*, we've made fonts, like cotton, the fabric of our lives.

Fun font factoids

The 50-foot letters of the famous Hollywood sign, originally erected in 1923, are the equivalent of a 43,200-point Arial font.

The Wicked Witch of the West's sky-written message, "Surrender Dorothy" (from *The Wizard of Oz* for those visiting from another planet), was the equivalent of 4,561,920-point Klang MT.

The Scarlet Letter "A" in the Nathaniel Hawthorne classic was the equivalent of 1,008-point Lucida Bright. The more discretely promoted phone number below it was 18-point Braggadocio.

"Daddy, what did you do in the sales downturn of '98?"

Belt-tightening—reducing expenses—is as important a contribution to the bottom line as a genuine sale (but without the overhead of morale). Here're some other ways to help the corporate ledger when your customers aren't buying:

- Apply for a government grant. Don't you watch those info-mercials? The government is giving away trillions of dollars just so they don't have to store it in a warehouse in Gaithersburg, MD, where the cost of renting a U-Store-It ri-vals that of a Manhattan co-op. A few programs for which you may want to apply for funding: efforts to reduce the number of homeless telecommuters, a plan to improve the OCR literacy rate, and, COBOL as a second language.

- Do something about skyrocketing health care costs. Direct your people to the luggage x-ray at the airport and cut your dental premiums dramatically.

- Don't even think about eliminating the annual holiday party—not when your local McDonald's PlayPlace is avail-able. The *hors d'oeuvres* may look a lot like toothpaste on a Cheese Nip, but who can complain when they get a toy with the main course?

- When you donate money to a charity, do so anonymously: don't sign the check.

- There are limits to how much you can squeeze out of your existing resources; after all, you can't get blood from a turnip, but you can get it from your staff. Let them think they're donating to the Red Cross, but you'll really be selling it to the local blood bank to fund the project T-shirts that read "Kwality at Any Cost!"

Hacked movie downloads

Warner Brothers announced last week that it would re-edit its classic *Cool Hand Luke* into a more contemporary version of the man vs. man vs. himself struggle.

In Luke '09, Paul Newman plays a similar character, but instead of doing hard time in a prison camp in the south, he plays a contract programmer for a California bank.

Strother Martin plays a network control technician who, in the midst of trouble-shooting a front-end processor, delivers the classic line, "What we've got here ... is failure to communicate."

It's not over until the fat lady shuts down

The operas we know and recognize today are not the same scores the composers originally penned. Here, restored from original backups, are some of the lost opera selections:

Wagner's **Die Walküre** premiered in Munich sans the selection *Das is not Ker Plunk*, in which Siegmund the Walsong rebukes the childlike application designs proposed by a programming intern. Wagner made a last-minute substitution having Wotan's daughter, Valkyrie Brünnhilde, bemoan her banishment to a three-week computer camp. Her arietta, *Mein Summer Kampf*, regrettably, was cut as well.

Verdi's **Il Trovatore** opened in Rome to a SRO audience of help desk personnel who literally brought down the house when they learned their favorite selection didn't make the final production: the gypsy Azucena was to sing, *fortissimo*, the ballad *Mi drive manga mi diskette ... so arriverderci accounts receivable*. No explanation was offered by the auditorium manager, but is was rumored that his advances to the singer were rebuffed, and he sought to limit her stage exposure.

Mozart's **Don Giovanni** opened in Prague, but the fire marshal was not standing by as originally penned. Wolfie had planned for the statue of Don Pedro to come to life, shuffle its feet across a carpet on the stage, and then point at Giovanni's motherboard producing an arc of static discharge large enough to illuminate the auditorium. It never happened, but opera buffs will recognize the obvious influence of Bessinni's tragic *Das Reboot*.

Don't quote me

"AhhGgg! Help Me! Help Me!
Jeez It Burns! It Burns!
Help Me! Please, Help Me!
AhhhhhhhGggg!"

—*Ben Franklin,*
discovering the first power surge

CyberClassifieds

For sale: Used modem, driven on the information superhighway only on Sundays by a little old lady logged on from Pasadena. frank@bennys-used-modems.com

Free to a good home page: Cute puppy clip art. jenny@ps121.edu

This is test post. Please ignore. john889152@aol.com

Will trade beer can collection for multimedia Pentium system. Plenty of primo cans. Many imports. circa-1974-user@hard-knox.edu

Business opportunity: Make up to $2000 a week formatting diskettes in your own home. Free info: money-money-money@more-money.con

Another business opportunity: Make $5000 a week locating lost relatives of wealthy, deceased Nigerian dignitaries. Visit www.ripsoffs.com and have your credit card ready.

Suspect a computer virus? Confidential testing and counseling available. Information at our FTP site: safehex.com Anonymous logins supported.

Government confiscated PCs from $3. Surplus Jeeps from $1. leo@not-exactly-the-gov.org

Are you overweight? Do you eat everything you see? We can help. Please visit our new web site: jerrys-online-chocolates.com

On not accounting for the time-difference when scheduling a teleconference ...

Getting ready to start a video-conference with my Australian IT counterpart, Uli Schmidt: "Uli, my friend, you are wearing pajamas, as well. Are you telecommuting from home today?"

"No, it's 3:30 A.M. I am *sleeping* from home."

All the news that's fit to feed

Analog storage comes "full circle"

RCA has announced that it expects to begin shipping their new *Full Circle* analog external storage silo by 2Q.

Because audio is converted from digital back to analog anyway, analog storage has been thought by some to be a practical alternative to conventional disk storage for many multimedia applications. "It's cheaper and in some cases faster," Richard Clarke, media reviewer for the cable TV show *StorageWeek*, said.

RCA has long been the leader in analog storage—their venerable 12-inch dual-sided disk can hold about 60 minutes of audio, something that would require almost 300 meg of digital storage. "But," says Clarke, "not having some sort of RAID implementation has prevented industry-wide acceptance."

To be sure, RCA had been touting their analog platter technology to hardware manufacturers for some time with little success, but it wasn't until they displayed a compact version at a trade show did they find a partner to help group the disks together to form a mass storage system.

Says RCA's Dolores Weiss, "When Wurlitzer Industries saw that our 7-inch compact version was 30 percent faster than the conventional disk—revolving at 45 revolutions per minute (RPMs) instead of $33^1/_3$—yet still stored several minutes of audio, they couldn't ink a deal with us to develop the *Full Circle* silo fast enough."

Wurlitzer's silo, marketed exclusively by RCA, will caddy 100 of the compact disks, each separately addressable by a keypad external to the device.

Asked how he might rate the new peripheral on his television show, Clarke said, "I haven't seen the technical specifications, but I'd give it a five because it's got a catchy title."

Ways to spot a net cruiser:

- They have fuzzy dice Windows wallpaper.

- They have a statue of St. Christopher on their terminal.

- They have a sub-woofer connected to their sound card.

- They collectively refer to their networked colleagues as their "convoy" and the data security officer as the "Smokey."

- Their screen-saver marquee reads, "If you don't like the way I navigate on the Information Superhighway ... STAY OFF THE BANDWIDTH."

Quality

When the operation's a success, but the patient dies

Don't ask Dallas-based Tropigala Foods why it's important to focus on quality. They're asking the same question. For seven years they've been developing an application to integrate all their IS functions. "Quality was priority #1," said Tropigala's Dave Heisinger, "we earmarked nearly a third of our project budget for code inspection and testing." But when they rolled out their million-line-plus defect-free "solution," users balked at the DOS program and its command-line interface. "We thought the feature-rich app would move like hotcakes," Heisinger said. "It did. It laid there on the shelf."

Beyond spell checking

Heisinger's problem is typical of application developers so tightly-focused on quality that they've lost touch with the end user. It's a natural slide. Rather than be innovative, developers look inwards and simply refine what they already have. This is not to say that today's apps can't benefit from a dose of quality, but 99 percent of quality initiatives have little impact on sales.

Today's "defect-oriented" quality paradigms are rooted in the manufacturing industry where quantitative data is easy to gather and interpret. Pareto Charts, Ishikawa diagrams, or other icons of the 90s-era quality Zeitgeist might be appropriate for tracking widget production, but when it comes to applications development or the service industry, in general, the only relevant metrics are last quarter's revenue figures.

Continuous improvement is admirable, but don't overestimate its impact on product success. Test cases don't determine quality, the user does.

One extreme's as bad as the other

Consider the saga of one software company's first post-ISO9000-detox offering: DenTech's patient database, touted as "the most user-friendly" of its type.

"When my client inadvertently initiated the program exit key-sequence," a court-appointed lawyer said in an opening statement, "he was taunted with a series of popup options which provoked the behavior for which he is accused."

The popups, referred to as *people's exhibit 1*, began innocuously enough, "Are you sure you would like to exit? Press OK or CANCEL."

When the user pressed the CANCEL button, the next pop up asked, "Are you sure you would like to cancel the exit? Press OK to CANCEL or CANCEL to EXIT." Pressing OK just drove a progressively more harassing panel as did the CANCEL button.

"Even with the nitrous oxide, it wasn't funny," orthodontist and beta tester Dr. Frank Switek testified.

Frustrated nearly to wits-end, Switek attempted to CNTL-ALT-DELETE out of the program, but when Windows asked if he really wanted to restart, he snapped and took a high-powered rifle up to the top of a nearby water tower for six hours before finally being talked down with the promise of a bottle of tangerine Frutopia and a new pair of Hush Puppies. Suffice to say, this is not the sort of pre-release customer feedback the developer was looking for.

Switek's tribulation highlights another programming mistake: developing a customer-oriented application with no user input at the design stage.

Surely DenTech was convinced it was doing the right thing. But they made the same arrogant assumption many other app developers make. They thought the user wanted a better mousetrap. If they bothered to ask they would have learned the user didn't have a rodent problem. They had termites.

The balancing act

On one side are the Deming-zealots singularly-focused on perfection defined as *adherence to specifications*; on the other are the marketeers with their finger on the pulse of the user's requirements. If you're unclear on which side to stand, put yourself in the user's ergonomic chair. Could *you* afford, in the Summer of '99, to wait thirty months for a zero-defect Y2K solution with an irrationally large number of testing resources verifying that the help panels contain grammatically correct text and the product's "custom install" is idiot-proof and executes without a hitch?

Well, if you've got two brain cells to rub together (I don't write this to make friends), you're saying, "I'll take the dangling participles and the 'hitches' if it means I have something I can work with NOW when I need it."

Certainly the product had better do what it's advertised to, but if your team is wasting cycles verifying help panel grammar, you're got way too

Case study: a sesquicentennial with no cause for celebration

For nearly 150 years, the Norwegian slide rule manufacturer, SlideRül, thrived. But a defect discovered in their popular Pentheus-Theda-7 triggered an unrecoverable six-sigma downward spin.

In 1969, a BMW engineer observed the "4" on his Theda-7's C-scale was etched .2 millimeters towards the "5," impacting nearly 30% of all floating-point calculations. SlideRül's reaction was to initiate a three-year quality program. But during that time, competitors took advantage of the defect with negative advertising campaigns like "20/4 = 5 on our slide rules. Can your rule make the same claim?" and frontal attacks like "SlideRül's 25% discount is really only 22.77%—they do the math on their Theda-7."

Thus began a features battle the outputs of which were the refinement of Teflon rails (for speed) and laser-etched scales (for precision).

SlideRül wasn't singularly-focused on quality, they *did* manage to look up from their workbench now and then. Unfortunately, it was just to eye the competition, not the market which had quickly become enamored with the new affordable pocket calculators. So when they released their Pentheus "M" series defect-free and on schedule in 1972, few noticed.

But SlideRül didn't care. Now they could calculate their losses to the fourth significant digit.

much free time.

That's why you need to commit now to look up from your terminal. Renounce the traditional definition of quality. And all its unnecessary work; and its empty promises.

Take the first step and include the user in your development cycle. It's a brave new paradigm, but consider the benefits:

- Letting the user help in the test phase eliminates wasted testing cycles. What sense does it make for those involved in the development process to inspect or test the finished product? Clearly if the developers think enough to test for a particular condition, they thought to code for it. More to the point, users are purposeful testers. They'll identify the functions critical to them and never notice the less-important ones; whereas developers typically attach the same importance to *all* operational areas.

- Incorporating user requirements in an application's design makes customers feel more like business partners, appreciating and evangelizing your efforts. This is the only way to know you're developing a quality product: one the user really wants

Is the customer always right? No, but there's little consolation in being on the moral high-ground while your app is sitting in the $4.99 bin at CompUSA.

All the news that's fit to feed

**What if They Held an Expo and Nobody Came?
Disgruntled Developers Get Answer**

Ex-Developer's Expo Opens to Lukewarm Crowd of Forty

Irvine, Calif. Jim Ekman had an idea while working in the R&D offices of Amana one afternoon. His wife phoned reporting the status of a cold their young son had caught. "I think he has a fever," Mrs. Ekman said. "His forehead feels warm."

Ekman asked the boy's temperature.

"I'm not sure," she said, "I can't find our thermometer."

In the true spirit of his help-desk background, Ekman vowed to get back to her "within the hour."

He soon called with a patch for the code that controlled the temperature probe of the family Radarange. Code that he authored. His wife merely needed to zap the chip via a handy utility he taught her to use in preparation for such an event.

"Just slip the probe under the boy's tongue," he said matter-of-factly.

"But he's much too young for an oral thermometer," she protested.

For the boy's delicate anatomy, Ekman needed to traverse the other end of the spectrum. "No problem," he said, "Zap the field from 'D6D9C1D3' to 'C2E4E3E3.'"

The quick and dirty was successful and happily the lad had only a slight fever .

Impressed with his handiwork, Ekman submitted it to his manager as an enhancement to the probe's op code.

Nonplussed, Ekman's manger relegated him to the shipping department where he was charged with inventory of the styrofoam packing peanuts. Ekman soon after resigned.

"Now I'm here," he said, "At this expo for the coolly received. Trying to sell my bells and whistles. But no one's listening. No one's here."

Indeed attendance at the first annual "Exposition for Unappreciated Developers" was poor.

"I take the blame." Mitch Piwak, Ex-Expo organizer said. "We scheduled it the same day as the local Consumer Electronics Show and you know they always have those porn stars signing autographs."

But audience or no audience, Piwak says, "It's going great. And I'm calling it a whooping success."

Weekend coder Nathan deRosa is also pleased. "I've licensed my hex to decimal conversion routine to three defense contractors," he said from behind his booth offering me a cup of cold coffee and an Andes candy. "My routine has its limitations—it can only handle a single-byte hex integer between zero and nine as input—but the aerospace people thought it was very slick."

For Frank Smuda, though, the expo has yet to justify his $85 booth rental investment. Slaving for twelve years writing code for GM's Buick division, Smuda knows some routines are harder to sell than others.

"I wrote the code that reminds the driver to fasten his seat belts, and the code that calculates trip-mileage," he boasted. "If you don't believe it, put your '89 Riviera into reverse and push the rear window de-fogger and cruise control resume button simultaneously—my initials are displayed on the digital speedometer. I wrote a lot of great routines for Buick, but when I submitted the computer-controlled intruder program (see illustration on following page), they gave me my walking papers. These people have no vision."

The expo continues through Sunday.

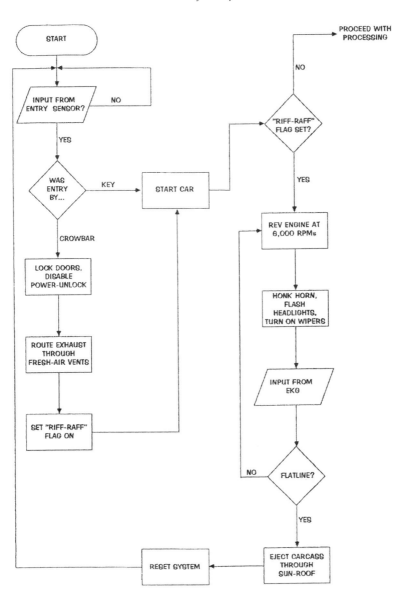

The subroutine that cost Smuda vesting in his company's 401k program.

One of the more "helpful" error messages:

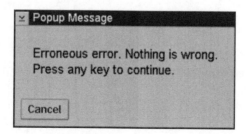

Electronic publishing: you make the call

No trees were harmed in the production of this column

Print this column and mail or fax it to everyone you know. Spread the word and help facilitate a paperless society.

You see, electronic publishing is hot and many veteran publications have developed web-versions of their periodicals—some have even totally replaced their old "hard copy" format with online content.

The good news is that there's less mail for the post office to handle.

The bad news is that downsized postal employees now have more time to devote to their hobby of gun collecting.

The "spate" of the art

It's difficult to say exactly why there's a rush to get a web presence. Some publications actually belong here. For example, technology publications *should* exploit the medium as should news organizations who can provide more current content electronically.

But this column's not about good web presence. It's about debunking the myth that anything worth doing should be done on the web.

Don't drip day-old vending machine coffee on my leg and tell me it's raining

Sorry, www.cyber_maui.com is *not* "the next best thing to actually being in Hawaii" as it claims. In fact, on the list of "next best things to actually being in Hawaii," swimming in a public pool in Scranton and dangling your feet off a commercial pier in Bayonne come up higher (6,521th and 11,214th on the next best things list, respectively) than *surfing* www.cyber_maui.com. But I digress.

Traditional periodicals lose a lot in the translation. And while readers might visit, the jury's still out as to whether or not they'll bookmark.

Consider some comments that came out of a focus group reviewing various online periodicals:

- "I just don't get the 'magazine experience' unless fifteen subscription cards fall out while I'm reading it."
- "I like it, don't get me wrong, but there's something about rolling up a newspaper and whacking your dog after he's dropped a torpedo on the rug, and ... and, how can I say this, I just don't see using the electronic version of the *Chicago Tribune* for that purpose."
- "It doesn't *smell* like *Cosmo* ... it's missing something ... I know, those perfume samples."
- "Personally, I think this is a crappy idea. And I'm not just saying that as a reader of old *TV Guides*, I'm saying that as a *collector* of old *TV Guides*."
- "Yes, I'll give you that *B.C.* is much funnier online, but it loses its utilitarian function as a bird cage liner in that medium."
- "Y'know, it's just not Miss September without the staples."

Can computers replace everything?

Probably.

But should they?

Won't we lose some of the artistry of the medium? When IBM's Deep Blue beat-out a virtual Elvis Stojko for a silver metal in Nagano who among us didn't wince at innocence lost?

OK, now raise you hand if you thought the little virtual

Zamboni that came out between programs was pretty cool.

Sure, electronic publishing offers opportunities to augment traditional print mediums, but in the words of Effram Zumatto[2], "The dream of a paperless society can never be realized until there is a way to do the *New York Times* crossword puzzle in the men's room."

---

[2] **For more information on Electronic Publishing ...** Effram Zumatto's 1,350-page seminal *Towards the Paperless Society* is now available in a special leather-bound edition printed on Brazilian rain forest paper. Ask your local bookseller for details.

MILESTONES IN THE HISTORY OF COMPUTING

Shakespeare's undeleted soliloquy

It is common knowledge that Shakespeare was a prolific writer. But a secret to all but the most astute computer history buffs is the Bard's greatest comedy/tragedy: the documentation for a CICS online application of the time.

Unfortunately, because of its propensity to crash at any hour of the night, the online was coined "A Midsummer Night's Downtime" and was quickly shelved.

Truly a greater tragedy was the loss of the original documentation, though scholars of the time apparently archived at least one menu prompt for posterity:

> *"To logoff or not to logoff, that is the question.*
> *What is your answer?*
> *Enter Y to proceed with session termination."*

Soap opera update

As The Disk Drives
Improprieties abound at Barton-Tech.

Thursday, Jolene was caught updating her résumé on the company PC just one day after Tony was reprimanded for pilfering coffee packets from the break-room.

In the MIS department, things got interesting when Perry inadvertently copied *Leisure Suit Larry* onto the backup copy of Barton-Tech's accounts receivables. When the episode closed, Baron Barton had just experienced a head crash and was walking towards Perry's office to get the backup for his restore. Look for Charlie to mysteriously arrive from Dallas with a new file recovery utility and save the company from a Chapter 11.

All My Upgrades
Denouncing "Jr." as a *bourgeois* epithet, yuppie Peter Norton wanna-be Thomas named his illegitimate son Thomas 2.0.

General Error
Harrison gave his two-week notice at SLIPDISC, and Frank finally laid it on the line for his estranged daughter. Just before breaking away for a Computer Learning Center commercial, he bellowed, "By God, Sarah, if you insist on going Macintosh, you're out of the will."

Am I the only one who misses Sam the custodian?

Gridlock on the information superhighway

If you thought an e-mail auto-responder was a time saver, don't look for the router at King Syndicates to concur. King, the agency that distributes the popular national column *Ethel Etiquette*, recently went into a hard-loop, disabling Internet traffic there for the entire afternoon.

Apparently, it all started when Ethel, who in real life is Schenectady, New York's Murray Harrabruda, received a scathing e-mail from rival columnist *Pamela Protocol* (Burt Meineike, of Toledo, Ohio). Ethel's autoresponder was programmed to automatically reply, "You're so kind" to any incoming message. Pamela's system answered incoming e-mail similarly with, "Nice of you to say so." The exchange then programmatically escalated to a recursive loop of "Thank you" and "Don't mention it." After almost 300,000 exchanges in four hours, King had to pull the plug on their network.

The $11-an-hour CIO

If you're going to sell your soul, at least haggle!

Hearken back to your humble beginnings and recall how easily you were deceived by the trappings of success:

It's 1977, and you've just been promoted to McDonald's crew chief. You can finally afford to buy your neighbor's old avocado-green '71 Ford Maverick. Maybe you bought a pair of Sedgefields to celebrate, as well.

Cruising the streets of Phoenix blasting Bob Seger through two blown rear speakers—your thick shoulder-length hair blowing in the wind from the passenger window that wouldn't close all the way because the crank broke in your brother's hand—man, you thought you had it made.

But of course, now you know better. Your newly leased Acura is leaps and bounds ahead of that rust bucket—both in performance and prestige. And your high-back oxblood office chair is a lot more comfortable than the Earth Shoes you stood in all afternoon while manning the fry machine.

You're at the top of your game, making, depending on which salary survey you believe, maybe low-six-figs a year. A far cry from the days you supplemented your income by selling bottle rockets out of your trunk. But are you really better off?

Well, if money is any gauge of success, it's time to crunch some numbers.

40 hours on Jupiter, maybe

Somewhere between the Maverick and the Acura, your work psyche has been branded "Bar-K-40-Hour-Workweek." And make no mistake, though the pain has long subsided, you still feel the burn. But be honest, when's the last time you worked *only* 40 hours in a week?

Have you ever, for instance, began your day not thinking about what awaits you at the office? How many family breakfasts have you sat through catatonic, even while Jr.'s sleeves dipped into the syrup of his pancakes or Suzie splashed grape juice on your new slacks?

We could micro-analyze your entire day, but to what end? You know that from 6:00 A.M. when you begin planning, until 6:00 P.M., when you finally call it a day, you're working, organizing, or fuming.

So what's that? A 60-hour workweek?

Oh, if it were just that. Remember that little *coup* you pulled with your developers? You got them to work through lunch just by popping for pizza. You spent maybe $30 for five pizzas and got seven $40-an-hour developers to work through lunch. Talk about ROI.

Sorry to burst your bubble, but you're not the first to come up with something like that. You know that high-end notebook your company gave all the managers and executives? Well, it wasn't so you could take it home and play Klondike. In fact, you probably spend two hours a night working from home, and another four to eight on the weekend.

You can see where this is going. So there's no need to dwell on it. Conservatively, then, you're looking at a 76-hour workweek.

But before you start bragging that $27-an-hour is still better than spending a half-hour a night washing the minimum-wage grease out of your hair, read on ...

Only two things are for sure, and one is just slightly worse than the other

National Tax Freedom Day is a symbolic day each year when you begin to keep the money your earn with regards to the taxes you pay. In Connecticut, for example, where taxes reign highest, the first

152 days of the year, or 42 percent of your salary, go towards various taxes. The average is 128 days, or 35 percent.

No one wants to dwell on taxes any longer than they have to, so suffice to say, you see about $17.50 for every hour you work.

Plumbing's starting to look like a good profession.

There's more coming out of your pocket than lint!

Here's the big one: unreimbursed out-of-pocket expenses. Check all that apply:

- ☐ You order in, working through lunch.

- ☐ You take your management team out to a lunch meeting; the accounting department kicks back your expense report because dessert is not authorized unless a customer is present. Rather than take the time to resubmit it, you eat the cost yourself.

- ☐ Your company reluctantly permits personal phone calls when necessary; however, they have a block on all 900-numbers. Your spouse happens to work at a Psychic Hotline, so the $3.99 a minute it costs to tell her that you're working late is entirely your responsibility.

- ☐ To keep up, you buy a steady stream of *schlemiel* books like *READ.ME Files for Dummies* and *The Complete Idiot's Guide to YES/NO Prompts*. Sure, you probably could get reimbursed, but then everyone in accounts payable would giggle when they see you.

- ☐ Guilt-gifts. You buy them at the airport when returning from a business trip. A $70 LEGO starter set for your son; a $35 box of Peanut M&M's for your daughter. A $225 set of faux pearls for your better half. Not to mention the three doubles you down during the layover in Denver.

- ☐ Quality child care. It's hard enough concentrating on a Word document with that damn paper clip popping up every five minutes trying to help you, but stir in a loud pinch of preteen argument in the family room and you're stuck either refereeing or distributing a double-sawbuck to each of them for an afternoon at the mall.

Making use of the "backward-completion principle," you probably spend about $494 a week on non-reimbursable expenses. Congratulations, my friend. You've made it. You're pulling down $11-an-hour!

The new corporate model

Of course, it's silly to look at your career as an $11-an-hour job. It's not. What's happened to our industry is that all the jobs have been eliminated and replaced with responsibilities. Your compensation is, supposedly, commensurate with your responsibility. Some responsibilities, though, are higher maintenance than others, hence the need for "perks" like beepers, cell phones, and notebooks.

But there is a dichotomy in this model, and not everyone's gotten the message. Many corporate regimes, for instance, openly invite you to take your notebook home and work evenings and weekends, but God forbid you should do some personal web surfing on "company time." Further, you can update your project plan on the train home rather than "decompress," but if you get caught writing a check for your electric bill at the office, it's going to reflect on your performance review.

The boxes at the top of the org chart will come around eventually, to be sure, but in the mean time, take every opportunity to remind them that today's work responsibilities are holistic: work and home lives have synthesized, hopefully to the betterment of both.

When you're chided for using company resources like the photocopier, shredder, or men's room for personal use, respectfully counter with the time saved running (literally) to the corner Kinkos.

All that said, ask yourself again if you're that much better off now with your $11-an-hour career than when you started out.

With twenty-two years in the business, you didn't exactly set the world on fire, did you?

Then again, when's the last time you had to push-start your Acura?

The nine categories of keycard photos

A statistic I have just made up suggests that the average professional has eleven employee access cards over the course of their career. Careful study of these reveals that all of the photos can be classified in one of the following categories:

1. "This is me when I tried a mustache." Nothing more needs to be said.
2. "The aberration." The foggy/grainy cross between a 7-11 surveillance camera photo and a special effect from *The Abyss*.
3. "Look at me, I'm a J.C. Penney model!" Again, no elaboration necessary.
4. *Rosemary's Baby*. An otherwise nice picture were it not for the red eye.
5. "The Secret." The photo presumably so unflattering that only the card reader has seen it; its holder wears it backwards on a lanyard and is quick to turn it face down on the desk when colleagues enter their cubicle.
6. "The Tintype." It's not your high school yearbook photo, but it might as well be because everyone who sees it says, "Good God, how old is that picture?"
7. The "Gee, look what's in my interoffice mailbox: the ID card I lost two days ago." Anonymously returned after being "retouched" with blacked-out teeth, geek glasses, and an Afro.

8. "The acquitted soldering-iron assaulter." The creepy picture whose beady eyes follow you around as your view the card from various angles and in all likelihood will be the photo accompanying the newspaper account that ends with the phrase, "... before turning the gun on himself."

9. "The unfortunate celebrity resemblance." Usually to Saddam Hussein, R.E.M.'s Michael Stipe, or Chewbacca.

Before the *BOSSKEY* ...

Manager to programmer: "Why is it that every time I come in here, you're playing video games on the computer?"

Programmer: "Because the carpeting in the hall muffles your footsteps."

Windows shopping

What better way to report on the state of high-tech consumerism than to jump in and experience it for yourself?

Such was my mission. Would I, *Datamation* magazine asked, purchase various items both on the web and in traditional brick-and-mortar shops? I played along. "OK," I told them. They continued. I would then make various witty, often unfounded, conclusions that were, they assured me, the job of an industry analyst.

The mission parameters were few: the items purchased must represent a suite of products consumers have shown a tendency to buy on the web. No sex stuff. "Not that we're prudes," my editor explained, "we just already have a lot of that ... data." One of the items would have to be steak because "we think that would be funny." And, finally, I would have to accomplish all of this on a budget of $75, which almost guaranteed the steak would have, in life, unsuccessfully run at Hialeah.

So, I hit the highways, both Interstate and Information, to deliver to you, the readers, the state of commerce.

Where's the beef?

It's never a good idea to begin your research on an empty stomach—unless you're studying the effects of bulimia. As it happened, I was getting hungry so I embraced this one.

While it's no secret that I was not born with the refined palette necessary to distinguish a Dom Pérignon '55 from a Colt .45, I *do* know my steak. And now that the high-protein, low-carbohydrate diet has lifted the red-meat guilt embargo, we can discuss beef—which has for too long been missing from the vocabulary of the learned—in mixed company, anyway.

So with stomach growling and the charcoals warming, I hit the web, found a site with some high-resolution pictures of steaks, and selected an attractive package of four 8-oz. USDA Prime rib eyes for the haughty "on sale" price of $44.95, plus $10.95 for shipping. For a pricey steak, you can do no better than Morton's or Ruth's Chris, but, I thought, what the heck, it was *Datamation's* money. Suffice to say, the service was poor. They took *forever* to get here (two days), and when they did arrive, they were cold.

To get a good steak, my grandmother used to say, you have to go to Pavel the Butcher. Unfortunately, Pavel has been dead for thirty years, but grandma's point was not lost on me. For fresh, quality meats, patronize your neighborhood butcher. Sadly, as mega-markets undercut them, neighborhood butchers are getting harder to find than an original company mission statement.

In our town, we have just one butcher shop, quaintly called, "Ye Olde Butcher Shoppe," run by a man that my wife and I call "Lazar Wolf," although we suspect he is of Norwegian descent. The shop is so well hidden in the slough (yes, I meant to spell it that way) of modern businesses, "Ye Olde" was indeed hard to find. I spent fifteen minutes searching for the place, and at times I was driving my car so slow that Amish people passing me in their carts were flipping me off.

In any event, it was worth the trip as I scored four mouth-watering, inch-thick, 8-oz., freshly cut Black Angus rib eyes for just $16.54. Even factoring in the mileage (14.4 miles at 32.5¢ cents per mile), it was far cheaper and more convenient to buy locally. (Note: I've eliminated time as a cost factor since there are far more useless ways to pass time. Staff meetings come to mind.)

Did e-commerce make the *cut*? (Note: I also considered the meat pun: Did e-commerce make the *grade*?) Decide for yourself:

- E-commerce downside: speed and cost
- E-commerce upside: accumulation of frequent flier miles if you have one of those credit cards that reward spending

- Local brick-and-mortar upside: speed and cost
- Local brick-and-mortar downside: butcher's hairy fingers

Buy the book

These days, no one would even consider buying a book without first checking for it at that online warehouse with the name of the big South American river.

So when the "coveted" (at least according to my eight-year-old) new Harry Potter book was announced, it was off to Big-SouthAmericanRiver.com where *The Goblet of Fire* was selling for 30 percent off its $25.95 list price plus, unfortunately, $4.29 shipping and a four-day wait, which, to an eight-year-old, is like four days of time-management orientation to us.

We needed that book *post haste*.

We could have paid list at our local pretentious bookseller. You know, the one where you need to carry a Starbucks cup around just to browse the four-wheeler magazines.

But list price was way beyond what my son's budget could sustain.

Instead, we got our copy at one of those mega-mart stores day-one for $12.97 plus $1.69 for a copy of *National Examiner*, which had a headline just too compelling to pass on—a mainframe computer claims it was a photocopier in a previous life.

Ours was a unique experience—finding a popular book in a mega-mart's one-aisle book section, that is. For more obscure tomes, the place to shop is online.

> **Loiterer's tip:**
>
> Bring your own Starbucks cup to the pretentious bookstore and fill it with the beverage of your choice. I find a *grande latte* cup filled with Bud makes the impromptu poetry readings inflicted on customers almost bearable.

Oops! ... I embarrassed myself again

Though Napster and its ilk are credited with declining CD sales, the truth is that many people are buying their CDs online.

Armed with my faithful barometer of whazzzzup, *Entertainment Weekly*, I needed to hear what the enlightened consider to be tragically hip nowadays. Well, regardless of *that* survey, I was about to purchase Santana's *Supernatural* until my eleven-year-old chimed in with, "No way, get Britney's *Oops!... I Did It Again*. Five million people can't be wrong," (the success of the Macarena would appear to disprove that).

So it was off to another one of the mega-mart stores, which I can't mention except that it starts with a "K." A very Big K.

I thought I would feel like a letch toting the 'tween CD. So I handed my son a twenty and sent him in because, after all, it was his idea. Fifteen minutes later he came out with a smirk only someone with an eleven-year-old would understand.

"My change?"

"What change?"

"Lemme see the receipt. OK, the CD was $15.92 ... and what would this '10 @ .39' be?"

As he slowly drew package after package of Wacky Wafers from his sweatshirt pocket, I realized how compelling point-of-sale promotions can be and how they can add to the total purchase price of the *intended* item (*déjà vu: National Examiner* incident)!

"OK, so the CD cost me twenty bucks."

"No, less than that," he said. "I found a penny in the parking lot ... here, you can have it."

Buying the CD online was much easier. Two button clicks, no guilt, four days, and $16.27 later I had my own Britney CD, which I have appropriately shelved next to my old Jerry Lee Lewis cassette in a box in the garage.

CD purchase *postmortem:* A phenomenon I'll coin, the "embarrassment factor," surfaced, which gives an edge to online pseudo-anonymous shopping.

Insert your own *double entendre* here.

Baseball cards been a-berry-berry good to me

Of course, not everything you need to purchase is available in local stores. Try buying a Beta copy of *The Dirty Dozen* or a Bachman-Turner Overdrive 8-track at Target. For these specialty items, you might spend weeks scouring the flea markets and local thrift stores.

Or you can boot up the Packard-Bell and do some Windows shopping. Online you'll find a greater selection of odd items at, typically, better prices. For instance, I found a 1969 Topps Roberto Clemente baseball card in "good" condition (meaning average wear) at a local shop selling for $55. I found a similarly-graded Roberto Clemente on eBay starting at $12. Eventually, I won the card for $31. When it arrived, though, the "average wear" included a goatee, blackened teeth, and devil horns.

Buying sight unseen: *caveat emptor!*

Brick-and-mortar vs. e-shopping

If you're looking for a victor, you won't find one.

Shopping is an experience. For some, that means wading through the stacks at a classic bookstore with a cup of fine brew steaming in your free hand. For others, it's a social event shared with friends. For many, it's simply utilitarian: zip in, zip out.

Online shopping adds a new dimension to the experience, both in convenience and selection.

The bottom line (or second line to the bottom depending on your browser width) is that neither will displace the other. Rather, they'll complement one another.

Sample dialog:

> **Brick-and-mortar shop:** "Gee, Mr. E-commerce site, may I compliment you on your great approach—large selection, no long checkout lines with someone without ID writing a check ahead of you, and the privacy and convenience of shopping without having to leave the comfort of your ergonomic seat."

> **E-commerce site:** "Well, thank you for those kind words, Mr. Brick-and-mortar shop. Might I say you have some mighty fine attributes yourself: speed, customer service, and ambiance. Now, if you would just do something about that acronym ..."

Grant comes in nick of time

M.o.I.T., Massachusetts' Other Institute of Technology, is celebrating for the first time since full-motion video was incorporated into *Tomb Raider*.

The normally austere academia is lauding a generous research grant to study bosskey technology in voice-recognition environments. Boss keys were originally developed in the early '80s so game-playing employees could hit a hot-key and instantly switch their monitors to display authentic looking business applications when a manager happened by. The grant supports the institute's research to develop a voice-recognition trigger to literally "call up" a faux-spreadsheet without alerting approaching management. Early progress has been reported with the phrase, "Ahem."

The grant comes at a time when the Institute was in desperate need of money. "You have to understand," Professor Lindenbrook of the computer science department said, "not having had a grant for some time, we were *this close* to shutting down." The staff was down to their last packet of coffee and was sneaking the sugar for it from a nearby Burger King.

"The grant bred new respect into us all. I used to hold a chair in the department of information engineering," associate professor Dr. Skoal said. "Now we can afford to get that chair fixed."

Time management: the last word

Quality time is for the office, not for your family. Go to work, do your job as efficiently as possible, then get the hell out of there and spend *quantity* time with the people you love.

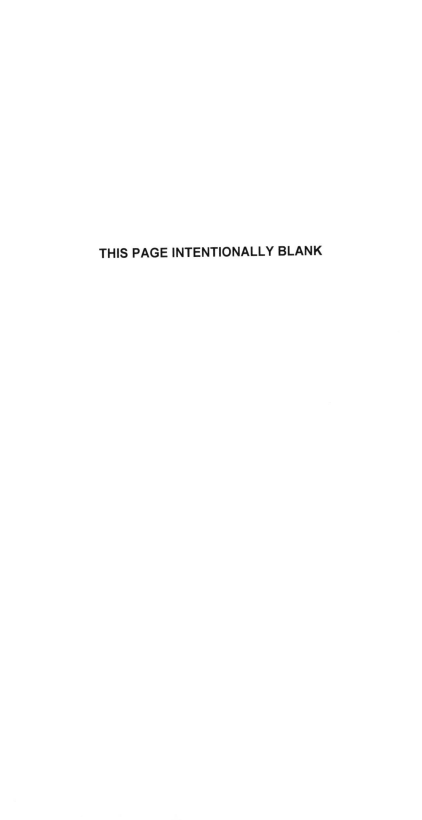
THIS PAGE INTENTIONALLY BLANK

...NOT SURE WHAT HAPPENED HERE

24748089R00091

Made in the USA
Middletown, DE
05 October 2015